PENGUIN POPULAR REFERENCE

FRENCH PHRASE BOOK

D0587981

French
Phrase
Book

SECOND EDITION

Henri Orteu and
Jill Norman

PENGUIN BOOKS

Published by the Penguin Group
Penguin Books Ltd, 80 Strand, London WC2R 0RL, England
Penguin Putnam Inc., 375 Hudson Street, New York, New York 10014, USA
Penguin Books Australia Ltd, Ringwood, Victoria, Australia
Penguin Books Canada Ltd, 10 Alcorn Avenue, Toronto, Ontario, Canada M4V 3B2
Penguin Books India (P) Ltd, 11 Community Centre, Panchsheel Park, New Delhi – 110 017, India
Penguin Books (NZ) Ltd, Cnr Rosedale and Airborne Roads, Albany, Auckland, New Zealand
Penguin Books (South Africa) (Pty) Ltd, 24 Sturdee Avenue, Rosebank 2196, South Africa

Penguin Books Ltd, Registered Offices: 80 Strand, London WC2R 0RL, England

www.penguin.com

First published 1968
Second edition 1978
11

Copyright © Jill Norman and Henri Orteu, 1968, 1978
All rights reserved

Printed in England by Cox & Wyman Ltd, Reading, Berkshire

Contents

6 Contents

Introduction

In this series of phrase books only those words and phrases that are essential to the traveller have been included. For easy reference the phrases are divided into sections, each one dealing with a different situation.

Some of the French phrases are marked with an asterisk * – these attempt to give an indication of the kind of reply you may get to your questions and of questions you may be asked.

At the end of the book is an extensive vocabulary list and here a pronunciation guide is given for each word. In addition there is an explanation of French pronunciation at the beginning of the book and a brief survey of the essential points of grammar. It would be advisable to read these sections before starting to use the book.

For those who would like to study the phrases and perfect their pronunciation, a further aid is available in the form of two 90-minute cassettes which contain all the words and phrases spoken clearly and distinctly by French men and women.

A leaflet giving full details is available from The Institute of Tape Learning, P.O. Box 4, Hemel Hempstead, Hertfordshire (tel. Hemel Hempstead (STD 0442) 68484).

Pronunciation

The pronunciation guide is intended for people with no knowledge of French. As far as possible the system is based on English pronunciation. This means that complete accuracy may sometimes be lost for the sake of simplicity, but the reader should be able to understand French pronunciation, and make himself understood, if he reads this section carefully. In addition, each word in the vocabulary is given with a pronunciation guide.

VOWELS

French vowels are much purer than English.

a	as 'a' in apple	symbol a	famille – fa-mee
ai,e	as 'e' in pen	symbol e	mettre – metr
			vinaigre – vee-negr
é,er	as 'ay' in pay	symbol ay	élastique – ay-las-teek
			marcher – mar-shay
è,er	as 'ai' in pair	symbol ai	père – pair
			travers – tra-vair
eu+l,r	not an English sound, but it is a little like the sound in 'her'	symbol œ	beurre – bœr
			seul – sœl

e,eu	this is like the vowel sound in 'the'	symbol e^r	le, je – le^r, zhe^r mercredi – mair-kre^r-dee
i	as 'ee' in meet NB i before e is usually pronounced 'y'	symbol ee	merci – mair-see fermier – fair-myay
o	as 'o' in olive	symbol o	poste – post pomme – pom
ou	as 'oo' in moon .	symbol oo	ouvert – oo-vair tout – too
u	not an English sound; round the lips and push them forwards as though to say 'oo' and try to say 'ee'	symbol u^e	rue – ru^e musée – mu^e-say
au,o	as 'oh'	symbol oh	chaud – shoh eau – oh
oi	as 'wa'	symbol wa	voiture – vwa-tu^{e}r
ui	as 'we'	symbol we	pluie – plwee oui – we

NASALS

These sounds should be made through the nose, but without pronuncing the 'n'.

an (m)	symbol ah^n	vent – vah^n
en (m)		manger – mah^n-zhay
on (m)	symbol oh^n	on – oh^n
		pont – poh^n
ain (m)	symbol a^n	faim – fa^n

Pronunciation 13

in (m)			vin – va^n
			bien – bya^n
un (m)		symbol e^n	brun – bre^n
			un – e^n

CONSONANTS

ch	as 'sh' in ship	symbol sh	chercher – shair-shay
j,g+e,i	as 's' in pleasure	symbol zh	garage – garazh
g+a,o,u	as 'g' in good; in pronunciation guide 'g' is sometimes followed by 'h' to make this clearer		guide – gheed
gn	pronounced as 'n-y'	symbol n-y	peigne – pen-y
h	not pronounced – but sometimes aspirate		hôtel – otel
ill,ail, euill	pronounced as 'y'	symbol y	fille – fee-y
			ail – a-y
qu	always pronounced 'k' not 'kw' as in English	symbol k	qualité – ka-lee-tay
r	is rolled more than in English		
s	as 's' in sip	symbol s	sucre – su^{e}kr
	as 's' in visit	symbol z	visite – vee-zeet
	final 's' is not pronounced (unless the next word starts with a consonant or silent 'h')		

The final consonant of a French word is not normally pronounced. However, if the next word begins with a vowel or silent 'h', the final consonant is then pronounced as the first sound of that word, e.g. les Anglais – lay-zah^n-glay. This kind of liaison is indicated in the vocabulary.

French has no stress as in English. It has a musical inflexion which runs throughout a sentence rather than individual words. Syllables have more or less equal value (unlike English), although the last pronounced syllable is sometimes very lightly stressed. Avoid anything resembling strong English stress, but you can give a little weight to the end of French words.

Basic grammar

GENDER OF NOUNS

In French nouns are either masculine or feminine.

e.g. *m*
le livre (the book)
le train (the train)

f
la table (the table)
la route (the road)

PLURAL OF NOUNS

To form the plural most nouns add -s. Those ending in -eau, -eu, and some ending in -ou take -x; most ending in -al change to -aux.

sing
le coiffeur (the hairdresser)
le bateau (the boat)
l'animal (the animal)

pl
les coiffeurs (the hairdressers)
les bateaux (the boats)
les animaux (the animals)

THE DEFINITE ARTICLE (the)

	m	*f*
sing	le père (the father)	la mère (the mother)
pl	les pères (the fathers)	les mères (the mothers)

Before a singular noun beginning with a vowel or a silent 'h' le (*m*), la (*f*) become l'

l'hôtel (the hotel)   l'auto (the car)
l'homme (the man)   l'adresse (the address)

THE INDEFINITE ARTICLE (a, an)

	m	*f*
sing	un hôtel (a hotel)	une auto (a car)

THE PARTITIVE ARTICLE (some, any)

	m	*f*
sing	du (=de+le) beurre (some butter)	de la confiture (some jam)
pl	des (=de+les) biscuits (some biscuits)	des pommes (some apples)

ADJECTIVES

Adjectives agree with the nouns they describe in gender and number.
To form the feminine most adjectives add -e to the masculine.
To form the plural most adjectives add -s.

	m	*f*
sing	un camion vert (a green lorry)	une auto verte (a green car)
pl	des camions verts (green lorries)	des autos vertes (green cars)

Adjectives are usually placed after the noun, but there are some exceptions.

POSSESSIVE ADJECTIVES

These adjectives agree in gender and number with the object possessed.

	m	*f*	*pl*
my	mon passeport	ma valise	mes enfants
his, her, its	son „	sa „	ses „
our	notre „	notre „	nos „
your	votre „	votre „	vos „
their	leur „	leur „	leurs „

DEMONSTRATIVE ADJECTIVES (this, these, that, those)

	m		*f*	
sing	ce monsieur	this/that gentleman	cette dame	this/that lady
pl	ces hommes	these/those men	ces femmes	these/those women

Before a masculine singular noun beginning with a vowel or a silent 'h' cet is used instead of ce.

e.g. cet homme this/that man   cet arbre this/that tree

RELATIVE PRONOUNS (who, whom, which, that)

subject	qui	La rue qui mène à la gare	the street that leads to the station
object	que	L'hôtelier que je connais	the hotel keeper whom I know

PERSONAL PRONOUNS

subject		direct object		indirect object of a verb		preceded by a preposition
I	je	me	me	to me	me	moi
you	tu	you	te	to you	te	toi
he, it	il	him, it	le	to him, her, it	lui	lui
she, it	elle	her, it	la	to her, it	lui	elle
we	nous	us	nous	to us	nous	nous
you	vous	you	vous	to you	vous	vous
they *m*	ils	them *m, f*	les	to them *m*	leur	eux
they *f*	elles			to them *f*	leur	elles

Object pronouns are usually placed between the subject and the verb.

e.g.	Je le vois	I see him	Je l'aide	I help him, her, it
	Il me parle	he speaks to me	Nous les mangeons	we eat them

VERBS

Verb forms are too difficult to discuss in detail here, but we give present, future, and perfect tenses of the regular verb patterns, and some of the more common irregular verbs. The perfect tense is made up of the present tense of *avoir*, or sometimes *être*, with the past participle of the verb. The verbs that usually form the past tense with *être* are: aller, venir, arriver, partir, entrer, sortir, naître, mourir, devenir, rester.

The second person singular *tu* is only used when speaking to children, close friends or relatives, and animals. In all other cases use *vous*.

Être – *to be*

Present		*Future*		*Past*	
je suis	*I am*	je serai	*I shall be, etc.*	j'ai été	*I was/have been, etc.*

Present		*Future*	*Past*	
tu es	*you are*	tu seras	tu as été	
il/elle est	*he/she is*	il sera	il a été	
nous sommes	*we are*	nous serons	nous avons été	
vous êtes	*you are*	vous serez	vous avez été	
ils/elles sont	*they are*	ils seront	ils ont été	

Avoir – *to have*

Present		*Future*		*Past*	
j'ai	*I have*	j'aurai	*I shall have, etc.*	j'ai eu	*I had/have had, etc.*
tu as	*you have*	tu auras		tu as eu	
il/elle a	*he/she has*	il aura		il a eu	
nous avons	*we have*	nous aurons		nous avons eu	
vous avez	*you have*	vous aurez		vous avez eu	
ils/elles ont	*they have*	ils auront		ils ont eu	

REGULAR VERBS

Aimer – *to like*; verbs ending in -er

Present	*Future*	*Past*
j'aime	j'aimerai	j'ai aimé, etc.

tu aimes	tu aimeras
il aime	il aimera
nous aimons	nous aimerons
vous aimez	vous aimerez
ils aiment	ils aimeront

Finir – *to finish*; verbs ending in -**ir**

Present	*Future*	*Past*
je finis	je finirai	j'ai fini, etc.
tu finis	tu finiras	
il finit	il finira	
nous finissons	nous finirons	
vous finissez	vous finirez	
ils finissent	ils finiront	

Vendre – *to sell*; verbs ending in -**re**

Present	*Future*	*Past*
je vends	je vendrai	j'ai vendu, etc.
tu vends	tu vendras	
il vend	il vendra	
nous vendons	nous vendrons	
vous vendez	vous vendrez	
ils vendent	ils vendront	

IRREGULAR VERBS

Aller – *to go*

Present	*Future*	*Past*
je vais	j'irai	je suis allé
tu vas	tu iras	tu es allé

il va	il ira	il est allé
nous allons	nous irons	nous sommes allés
vous allez	vous irez	vous êtes allés
ils vont	ils iront	ils sont allés

Boire – *to drink*

Present	*Future*	*Past*
je bois	je boirai	j'ai bu, etc.
tu bois	tu boiras	
il boit	il boira	
nous buvons	nous boirons	
vous buvez	vous boirez	
ils boivent	ils boiront	

Connaître – *to know (someone)*

Present	*Future*	*Past*
je connais	je connaîtrai	j'ai connu, etc.
tu connais	tu connaîtras	
il connaît	il connaîtra	
nous connaissons	nous connaîtrons	
vous connaissez	vous connaîtrez	
ils connaissent	ils connaîtront	

Devoir – *to have to, must*

Present	*Future*	*Past*
je dois	je devrai	j'ai dû, etc.
tu dois	tu devras	
il doit	il devra	
nous devons	nous devrons	
vous devez	vous devrez	
ils doivent	ils devront	

Dire – *to say*

Present	*Future*	*Past*
je dis	je dirai	j'ai dit, etc.
tu dis	tu diras	
il dit	il dira	
nous disons	nous dirons	
vous dites	vous direz	
ils disent	ils diront	

Faire – *to make, do*

Present	*Future*	*Past*
je fais	je ferai	j'ai fait, etc.
tu fais	tu feras	
il fait	il fera	
nous faisons	nous ferons	
vous faites	vous ferez	
ils font	ils feront	

Lire – *to read*

Present	*Future*	*Past*
je lis	je lirai	j'ai lu, etc.
tu lis	tu liras	
il lit	il lira	
nous lisons	nous lirons	
vous lisez	vous lirez	
ils lisent	ils liront	

Mettre – *to put*

Present	*Future*	*Past*
je mets	je mettrai	j'ai mis, etc.
tu mets	tu mettras	

Present	*Future*	*Past*
il met	il mettra	
nous mettons	nous mettrons	
vous mettez	vous mettrez	
ils mettent	ils mettront	

Partir – *to leave*

Present	*Future*	*Past*
je pars	je partirai	je suis parti, etc.
tu pars	tu partiras	
il part	il partira	
nous partons	nous partirons	
vous partez	vous partirez	
ils partent	ils partiront	

Pouvoir – *to be able, can*

Present	*Future*	*Past*
je peux	je pourrai	j'ai pu, etc.
tu peux	tu pourras	
il peut	il pourra	
nous pouvons	nous pourrons	
vous pouvez	vous pourrez	
ils peuvent	ils pourront	

Prendre – *to take*

Present	*Future*	*Past*
je prends	je prendrai	j'ai pris, etc.
tu prends	tu prendras	
il prend	il prendra	
nous prenons	nous prendrons	
vous prenez	vous prendrez	
ils prennent	ils prendront	

Savoir – *to know (something)*

Present	*Future*	*Past*
je sais	je saurai	j'ai su, etc.
tu sais	tu sauras	
il sait	il saura	
nous savons	nous saurons	
vous savez	vous saurez	
ils savent	ils sauront	

Venir – *to come*

Present	*Future*	*Past*
je viens	je viendrai	je suis venu, etc.
tu viens	tu viendras	
il vient	il viendra	
nous venons	nous viendrons	
vous venez	vous viendrez	
ils viennent	ils viendront	

Voir – *to see*

Present	*Future*	*Past*
je vois	je verrai	j'ai vu, etc.
tu vois	tu verras	
il voit	il verra	
nous voyons	nous verrons	
vous voyez	vous verrez	
ils voient	ils verront	

Vouloir – *to want*

Present	*Future*	*Past*
je veux	je voudrai	j'ai voulu, etc.
tu veux	tu voudras	
il veut	il voudra	
nous voulons	nous voudrons	
vous voulez	vous voudrez	
ils veulent	ils voudront	

NEGATIVE

The negative is formed by putting **ne** before the verb and **pas** after. Ne becomes **n'** before a vowel.

e.g. Je ne suis pas   I am not French   Je n'ai pas   I've no money
      français   d'argent

Essentials

First things

Yes	Oui
No	Non
Please	S'il vous plaît
Thank you	Merci
You're welcome (*in reply to thanks*)	Je vous en prie/De rien
Yes, please	Oui, merci
No, thank you[1]	(Non) merci

---

1. In reply to an offer of any kind *merci* means 'no thank you'. To accept, one should say *oui, merci* or *oui, s'il vous plaît*.

Language problems

I'm English/American	Je suis anglais(-e)/américain(-e)
Do you speak English?	Parlez-vous anglais?
Does anybody here speak English?	Est-ce que quelqu'un parle anglais ici?
I don't speak (much) French	Je ne parle pas (bien) français
Do you understand (me)?	Est-ce que vous (me) comprenez?
I don't understand	Je ne comprends pas
Would you say that again, please?	Voulez-vous répéter, s'il vous plaît?
Please speak slowly	Parlez lentement, je vous prie
What does that mean?	Qu'est-ce que cela veut dire?
Can you translate this for me?	Pouvez vous me traduire ceci?
Please write it down	Écrivez-le, s'il vous plaît
What do you call this in French?	Comment appelez-vous ceci en français?
I will look it up in my phrase book	Je vais consulter mon manuel de conversation

Questions

Who?	Qui?
Where is/are . . .?	Où est/sont . . .?
When?	Quand?
How?	Comment?
How much is/are . . .?	Combien coûte/coûtent . . .?
How far?	C'est à quelle distance?
What?	Quoi?
What's that?	Qu'est-ce que c'est?
What do you want?	Que voulez-vous?
What must I do?	Que dois-je faire?
Why?	Pourquoi?
Have you . . .?	Avez-vous . . .?
Is there . . .?	Y a-t-il . . .?
Have you seen . . .?	Avez-vous vu . . .?
May I have . . .?	Pourrais-je avoir . . .?
I want/should like . . .	Je veux/voudrais . . .
I don't want . . .	Je ne veux pas . . .
What is the matter?	Qu'est-ce qu'il y a?
Can you help me?	Pouvez-vous m'aider?
Can I help you?	*Puis-je vous aider?
Can you tell/give/show me . . .	Pouvez-vous me dire/donner/montrer . . .

Useful statements

Here is/are ...	Voici ...
I like it	Je l'aime bien
I don't like it	Je n'aime pas ça
I know	Je sais
I don't know	Je ne sais pas
I didn't know	Je ne savais pas
I think so	Je crois que oui
I'm hungry/thirsty	J'ai faim/soif
I'm tired/in a hurry/ready	Je suis fatigué/pressé/prêt
Leave me alone	Laissez-moi tranquille
Just a minute	*Une minute/un instant
This way, please	*Par ici, s'il vous plaît
Take a seat	*Asseyez-vous
Come in!	*Entrez!
It's cheap	C'est bon marché
It's (too) expensive	C'est (trop) cher
That's all	C'est tout
You're right/wrong	Vous avez raison/tort

Greetings

Good morning/good day/ good afternoon	*when meeting* Bonjour monsieur/ madame/mademoiselle *when departing* Au revoir
Good evening	Bonsoir
Good night	*only when going to bed* Bonne nuit/*otherwise* Bonsoir
How are you?	Comment allez-vous?
Very well, thank you	Très bien, merci
Good-bye	Au revoir
See you soon	À bientôt
See you tomorrow	À demain
Have a good journey	Bon voyage
Have a good time	Amusez-vous bien
Good luck/all the best	Bonne chance

Polite phrases

Sorry	Pardon
Excuse me	Excusez-moi
That's all right (*in reply to* excuse me)	Il n'y a pas de mal/Ce n'est rien

Not at all/don't mention it (*after thanks*)	Il n'y a pas de quoi/je vous en prie
Everything all right?	(Est-ce que) tout va bien?
Can't complain	Ça va/Je ne peux pas me plaindre
Don't worry	Ne vous inquiétez pas
It doesn't matter	Cela ne fait rien/cela n'a pas d'importance
I beg your pardon? What?	Comment?
Am I disturbing you?	Est-ce que je vous dérange?
I'm sorry to have troubled you	Je suis désolé de vous avoir dérangé
Good/that's fine	Bien/c'est parfait
Thanks for your trouble	Merci du dérangement

Opposites

before/after	avant/après	a-vah^n/a-pre
early/late	tôt/tard	toh/tar
early (*ahead of schedule*)	en avance	ah^n a-vah^{n}s
late (*behind schedule*)	en retard	ah^n re^{r}tar
first/last	premier/dernier	pre^{r}m-yay/dair-nyay
now/later, then	maintenant/plus tard, alors	mah^{n}te^{r}nah^n/plu^{e}tar, a-lor

far/near	loin/près	lwan/pre
here/there	ici/là	ee-see/la
in/out	dans/hors de	dahn/or-de
inside/outside	à l'intérieur, dedans/à l'extérieur, dehors	a lan-tay-rœr, der-dah/a lek-stay-rœr, der-or
under/over	au-dessous/au-dessus	oh-der-soo/oh-der-sue
big, large/small	grand/petit	grahn/per-tee
deep/shallow	profond/peu profond	pro-fohn/per pro-fohn
empty/full	vide/plein	veed/plan
fat/lean	gras/maigre	gra/megr
heavy/light	lourd/léger	loor/lay-zhay
high/low	haut/bas	oh/ba
long, tall/short	grand/petit	grahn/per-tee
narrow/wide	étroit/large	ay-trwa/larzh
thick/thin	épais/mince	ay-pe/mans
least/most	le moins/le plus	ler mwan/ler plue
many/few	beaucoup/peu	boh-koo/per
more/less	plus/moins	plue/mwan
much/little	beaucoup/peu	boh-koo/per
beautiful/ugly	beau/laid	boh/le
better/worse	meilleur/pire	may-œr/peer
cheap/dear	bon marché/cher	bohn mar-shay/shair

clean/dirty	propre/sale	propr/sal
cold/hot, warm	froid/chaud	frwa/shoh
easy/difficult	facile/difficile	fa-seel/dee-fee-seel
fresh/stale	frais/pas frais	fre/pa fre
good/bad	bon/mauvais	bohn/moh-ve
new, young/old	nouveau, jeune/vieux	noo-voh, zhœn/vyer
nice/nasty	gentil/méchant	zhahn-tee/may-shahn
right/wrong	juste/faux	zhuest/foh
free/taken	libre/occupé	leebr/o-kue-pay
open/closed, shut	ouvert/fermé	oo-vair/fair-may
quick/slow	rapide/lent	ra-peed/lahn
quiet/noisy	calme/bruyant	kalm/brwee-ahn
sharp/blunt	pointu, (*of blade*)	pwantue, e-gee-zay/
	aiguisé/émoussé	ay-moo-say

Signs and public notices[1]

À louer	To let/for hire
À vendre	For sale
Ascenseur	Lift/elevator
Attention	Caution
Banque	Bank
Caisse	Cashier's desk
Chambre à louer	Room to let
Chambres libres	Vacancies
Commissariat de police[2]	Police station
Complet	Full/no vacancies/no seats
Dames	Ladies
Danger	Danger
Défense d'entrer	Private/no entry
Défense d'entrer sous peine d'amende	Trespassers will be prosecuted

1. See also MOTORING (p. 54)   2. See note, p. 153.

Défense de fumer	No smoking
Eau non potable	(Water) not for drinking
Eau potable	Drinking water
Entrée	Entrance
Entrée interdite	No admission
Entrée libre	Admission free
Entrez sans frapper	Please enter
Fermé	Closed
Frappez	Knock
Gendarmerie[1]	Police station
Guide	Guide
Interprète	Interpreter
Issue de secours	Emergency exit
Libre	Vacant/free/unoccupied
Messieurs	Gentlemen
Ne pas toucher	Do not touch
Occupé	Engaged/occupied
Ouvert de . . . à . . .	Open from . . . to . . .
P. et T.	Post Office
Passage interdit	No entry
Piétons	Pedestrians
Places debout seulement	Standing room only
Poussez	Push

1. See note, p. 153.

Prière de ne pas ...	You are requested not to ...
Privé	Private
Renseignements	Information
Réservé	Reserved
Soldes	Sale
Sonnez	Ring
Sortie	Exit
Sortie de secours	Emergency exit
Tenez votre droite	Keep right
Tirez	Pull
Toilettes	Lavatory/toilets

Abbreviations

A.	Autoroute	motorway
A.O.C.	Appellation d'origine controllée	highest classification for wine
apr. J.-C.	Après Jésus-Christ	A.D.
av. J.-C.	Avant Jésus-Christ	B.C.
Bd	Boulevard	boulevard
c.-à-d.	C'est-à-dire	i.e.
C.C.P.	Compte courant postal	giro account

C.E.E.	Communauté économique européenne	E.E.C.
C.H.U.	Centre hospitalier universitaire	teaching hospital
C.R.S.	Compagnies républicaines de sécurité	riot police
E.D.F.	Électricité de France	state electricity board
h.	Heure	hour
J.M.F.	Jeunesses musicales de France	association of young music lovers
m.	Minute, mètre	minute, metre
M.	Monsieur	Mr
M.J.C.	Maison des jeunes et de la culture	youth centre
Mlle	Mademoiselle	Miss
Mme	Madame	Mrs
O.N.U.	Organisation des Nations Unies	U.N.O.
O.R.L.	Oto-rhino-laryngologie	ear, nose and throat
O.R.T.F.	Office de la radiodiffusion et télévision françaises	French broadcasting service
O.V.N.I.	Objet volant non identifié	U.F.O.
p.c.	Pour cent	per cent
P. et T.	Postes et télécommunications (formerly P.T.T.)	Post Office
p. ex.	Par exemple	e.g.
P.M.U.	Pari mutuel urbain	tote (see page 135)

R.	Rue	street
R.A.T.P.	Régie autonome des transports parisiens	Paris transport authority
R.E.R.	Réseau express régional	fast suburban transport in Paris
R.F.	République française	French republic
R.N.	Route nationale	trunk road
s/	Sur	on (in place names)
/s	Sous	under (in place names)
S.A.R.L.	Société à responsabilité limitée	limited company
S.I.	Syndicat d'initiative	tourist information office
S.N.C.F.	Société nationale des chemins de fer français	French railways
T.C.F.	Touring club de France	French automobile association
t.t.c.	toutes taxes comprises	all taxes included
T.V.A.	Taxe sur la valeur ajoutée	V.A.T.
V.D.Q.S.	Vin délimité de qualité supérieure	second highest classification for table wine
Vve	Veuve	widow
Z.U.P.	Zone à urbaniser en priorité	development area

Money[1]

Is there a bank/an exchange bureau near here?	Y a-t-il une banque/un bureau de change près d'ici?
Do you cash traveller's cheques?	Acceptez-vous les chèques de voyage?
Where can I cash traveller's cheques?	Où puis-je encaisser des chèques de voyage?
I want to change some English/ American money	Je voudrais changer des livres sterling/des dollars
How much do I get for a pound/ dollar?	Combien vaut la livre/le dollar?
Can you give me some small change?	Pourriez-vous me donner de la monnaie?
Will you take a personal cheque?	Accepterez-vous un chèque?
Do you have any identification/ a banker's card?	*Avez-vous une pièce d'identité/ une carte bancaire?

1. In France most banks are open from 9 a.m. to 5 p.m. All banks are closed on Sundays. Some are closed on Saturdays, some on Mondays. In Switzerland they are open from 8 or 8.30 a.m. to 5 p.m., closed Saturday and Sunday. In Belgium they open from 10 a.m. to 12 noon, and from 2 to 4 p.m., closed Saturday and Sunday.

Sign here, please	*Signez ici s'il vous plaît
Go to the cashier	*Allez à la caisse
What is the current rate of exchange?	Quel est le taux de change?

CURRENCY

Belgium: 100 Centimes (ct)	=	1 F(ranc)
France: 100 Centimes (ct)	=	1 F(ranc)
Switzerland: 100 Centimes (ct)	=	1 F(ranc)

Travel

On arrival

Passport control	*Contrôle des passeports
Your passport, please	*Votre passeport, s'il vous plaît
Are you together?	*Vous êtes ensemble?
I'm travelling alone	Je voyage seul
I'm travelling with my wife/ a friend	Je voyage avec ma femme/ un(e) ami(e)
I'm here on business on holiday	Je suis ici pour affaires Je viens passer mes vacances
May I see your green card, please?	Pouvez-vous me montrer votre carte verte?
What is your address in Paris/ France?	*Quelle est votre adresse à Paris/en France?
How long are you staying here?	*Combien de temps pensez-vous rester?
How much money have you got?	*Combien d'argent avez-vous?

I have ... francs/pounds/dollars	J'ai ... francs/livres/dollars
Customs	*Douane
Goods to declare	*Quelque chose à déclarer
Nothing to declare	*Rien à déclarer
Which is your luggage?	*Quels sont vos bagages?
Do you have any more luggage?	*Avez-vous d'autres bagages?
This is my luggage	Voici mes bagages
That is all my luggage	Ce sont là tous mes bagages
Have you anything to declare?	*Avez-vous quelque chose à déclarer?
I have only my personal things in it	Il n'y a là que mes affaires personnelles
I have a carton of cigarettes and a bottle of gin/wine	J'ai une cartouche de cigarettes et une bouteille de gin/vin
Open your bag, please	*Ouvrez votre sac, s'il vous plaît
Can I shut my case now?	Puis-je refermer ma valise maintenant?
May I go through?	Puis-je passer?
Where is the information bureau?	Où se trouve le bureau de renseignements?
Porter!	Porteur!
Would you take these bags to a taxi/the bus?	Portez ces bagages jusqu'à un taxi/l'autobus, s'il vous plaît
What is the price for each piece of luggage?	C'est combien par colis?

I shall take this myself	Je porterai cela moi-même
That's not mine	Ce n'est pas à moi
How much do I owe you?	Combien est-ce que je vous dois?

Signs to look for at stations, etc.

Arrivals	Arrivée
Booking Office	Location
Buses	Autobus
Connections	Correspondances
Departures	Départ
Exchange	Change
Gentlemen	Messieurs
Information	Renseignements
Ladies' Room	Dames
Left Luggage { in / out	Consigne { dépôts / retraits
Lost Property	Bureau des objets trouvés
Luggage Lockers	Consigne automatique
Main Lines	Grandes lignes
Non-Smoker	Non-Fumeur
Platform	Quai
Refreshments	Buvette/Buffet

Reservations	Réservations
Smoker	Fumeur
Suburban Lines	Lignes de banlieue
Taxis	Taxis
Tickets	Billets
Underground	Métro (Métropolitain)
Waiting Room	Salle d'attente

Buying a ticket

Where's the nearest travel agency?	Où se trouve l'agence de voyage la plus proche?
Is there a tourist office?	Y a-t-il un office du tourisme?
Have you a timetable, please?[1]	Avez-vous un horaire, s'il vous plaît?
What's the tourist fare to . . .?	Combien coûte le billet touristique pour . . .?
How much is it first class to . . .?	Combien coûte un billet de première pour . . .?
A second class single to . . .	Un aller simple en deuxième classe pour . . .
Three singles to . . .	Trois aller simples pour . . .
A return to . . .	Un aller et retour pour . . .

1. The equivalent of the British 'ABC Rail Guide' is called 'Indicateur Chaix'.

Are there reduced rate tickets?	Y a-t-il des billets à tarif réduit?
Is there a special rate for children?	Y a-t-il un tarif spécial pour enfants?
How old is he/she?	*Quel âge a-t-il/a-t-elle?
How long is this ticket valid?	Combien de temps ce billet est-il valable?
A book of tickets, please[1]	Un carnet de tickets, s'il vous plaît
Is there a supplementary charge?	Y a-t-il un supplément à payer?

By train and underground

RESERVATIONS AND INQUIRIES

Where's the railway station/ tube station?	Où est la gare/la station de métro?
Where is the ticket office?	Où est le guichet de vente des billets?
Two seats on the ... to ...	Deux places pour ... dans le train de ...
I want to reserve a sleeper	Je voudrais réserver un wagon-lit
How much does a couchette cost?	Combien coûte une couchette?

1. This is only available for bus or tube journeys. It is much cheaper to buy a *carnet* than single tickets for each journey.

I want to register this luggage through to . . .	Je voudrais faire enregistrer ces bagages à destination de . . .
Is it an express or a local train?[1]	Est-ce un train express ou un omnibus?
Is there an earlier/later train?	Y a-t-il un train plus tôt/plus tard?
Is there a restaurant car on the train?	Ce train a-t-il un wagon-restaurant?

CHANGING

Is there a through train to . . .?	Y a-t-il un train direct pour . . .?
Do I have to change?	Dois-je changer de train?
Where do I change?	Où dois-je changer?
When is there a connection to . . .?	Quand y a-t-il une correspondance pour . . .?

DEPARTURE

When does the train leave?	À quelle heure part le train?
Which platform does the train to . . . leave from?	Sur quelle voie part le train pour . . .?
Is this the train for . . .?	Est-ce bien le train pour . . .?

1. Most de-luxe trains in France have a special name according to their destination — e.g. *Mistral* (Paris to Nice), *Capitole* (Paris to Toulouse). They are usually first class only.

ARRIVAL

When does it get to . . .?	À quelle heure arrive-t-il à . . .?
Does the train stop at . . .?	Est-ce que le train s'arrête à . . .?
How long do we stop here?	Combien dure l'arrêt ici?
Is the train late?	Est-ce que le train a du retard?
When does the train from . . . get in?	À quelle heure arrive le train de . . .?
At which platform?	Sur quelle voie?

ON THE TRAIN

We have reserved seats	Nous avons des places réservées
Is this seat free?	Est-ce que cette place est libre?
This seat is taken	*Cette place est occupée
Ticket inspector	Le contrôleur

By air

Where's the airline office?	Où se trouve l'agence de la compagnie aérienne?
I'd like to book two seats on the plane to . . .	Je voudrais réserver deux places dans l'avion à destination de . . .
Is there a flight to . . .?	Est-ce qu'il y a un vol à destination de . . .?

When does it leave/arrive?	À quelle heure est le départ/ l'arrivée?
What is the flight number?	Quel est le numéro du vol?
When's the next plane?	Quand part le prochain avion?
Is there a coach between the town and the airport?	Y a-t-il un service d'autocars entre la ville et l'aéroport?
When must I check in?	À quelle heure est l'enregistrement?
Please cancel my reservation to ...	Annulez ma réservation pour ..., s'il vous plaît
I'd like to change my reservation	Je voudrais changer ma réservation

By boat

Is there a boat/car ferry from here to ...?	Y a-t-il un bateau/car ferry pour ...?
How long does the boat take?	Combien dure la traversée?
How often do the boats leave?	Tous les combien partent les bateaux?
Does the boat call at ...?	Est-ce que le bateau fait escale à ...?
When does the next boat leave?	Quand part le prochain bateau?
Can I book a single berth cabin?	Puis-je réserver une cabine à une place?

How many berths are there in the cabin?	Combien de places y a-t-il dans la cabine?
When must we go on board?	À quelle heure devons-nous embarquer?
When do we dock?	À quelle heure accostons-nous?
How long do we stay in port?	Combien dure l'escale?

By bus or coach

Where's the bus station/coach station?	Où est la station d'autobus/ la gare routière?
Bus stop	*Arrêt d'autobus
Compulsory stop	*Arrêt fixe
Request stop	*Arrêt facultatif
When does the coach leave?	À quelle heure part l'autocar?
When does the coach get to . . .?	À quelle heure est-ce que l'autocar arrive à . . .?
What stops does it make?	Où est-ce qu'il s'arrête?
How long is the journey?	Combien dure le voyage/le trajet?
We want to take a coach tour round the sights	Nous voulons faire une visite touristique en autocar
Is there a sightseeing tour?	Y a-t-il un circuit touristique?
What is the fare?	Quel est le prix du billet?

Does the bus/coach stop at our hotel?	Est-ce que l'autobus/le car s'arrête à notre hôtel?
Is there an excursion to . . . tomorrow?	Est-ce qu'il y a une excursion à . . . demain?
When's the next bus?	À quelle heure est le prochain autobus?
How often do the buses run?	Quelle est la fréquence des autobus?
Has the last bus gone?	Est-ce que le dernier autobus est parti?
Does this bus go to the town centre/beach/station?	Est-ce que cet autobus va au centre de la ville/à la plage/ à la gare?
Do you go near . . .?	Allez-vous du côté de . . .?
Where can I get a bus to . . .?	Où puis-je prendre un autobus pour . . .?
Which bus goes to . . .?	Quel autobus va à (au) . . .?
I want to go to . . .	Je voudrais aller à (au) . . .
Where do I get off?	Où dois-je descendre?
The bus to . . . stops over there	*L'autobus pour . . . s'arrête là-bas
You must take a number . . .	*Il faut prendre le . . .
(You) get off at the next stop	*(Vous) descendez au prochain arrêt
The buses run every ten minutes/every hour	*L'autobus passe toutes les dix minutes/toutes les heures

By taxi

Please get me a taxi	Voulez-vous m'appeler un taxi, s'il vous plaît
Where can I find a taxi?	Où puis-je trouver un taxi?
Are you free?	Êtes-vous libre?
Please take me to the St Sulpice hotel/the station/this address	Conduisez-moi à l'hôtel Saint Sulpice/à la gare/à cette adresse, s'il vous plaît
Can you hurry, I'm late?	Pouvez-vous aller vite, je suis en retard
Please wait for me	Attendez-moi, s'il vous plaît
Stop here	Arrêtez-vous ici
Is it far?	C'est loin?
How much do you charge by the hour/for the day?	Combien coûte l'heure de location/la journée de location?
How much will you charge to take me to . . .?	Quel est le prix de la course pour aller à . . .?
How much is it?	Combien vous dois-je?
That's too much	C'est trop cher

Directions

Excuse me; could you tell me . . .	Pardon Monsieur/Madame/Mademoiselle; pouvez-vous me dire . . .
Where is . . .?	Où est . . .?
How do I get to . . .?	Comment fait-on pour aller à . . .?
How far is it to . . .?	À quelle distance se trouve . . .?
How many kilometres?	Combien de kilomètres?
How do we get on to the motorway to . . .?	Comment parvient-on à l'autoroute qui va à . . .?
Which is the best road to . . .?	Quelle est la meilleure route pour aller à . . .?
Is there a scenic route to . . .?	Y a-t-il un itinéraire touristique pour aller à . . .?
Where does this road lead to?	Où est-ce que cette route mène?
Is it a good road?	Est-ce que la route est bonne?
Is it a motorway?	Est-ce que c'est une autoroute?

Is there any danger of avalanches/snowdrifts?	Risque-t-il d'y avoir des avalanches/des congères?
Will we get to . . . by evening?	Pourrons-nous arriver à . . . dans la soirée?
Where are we now?	Où sommes-nous maintenant?
What is the name of this place?	Quel est le nom de cet endroit?
Please show me on the map	Montrez-moi où nous sommes sur la carte, s'il vous plaît
It's that way	*C'est de ce côté/C'est par là
It isn't far	*Ce n'est pas loin
Follow this road for 5 kilometres	*Suivez cette route sur cinq kilomètres
Keep straight on	*Allez tout droit
Turn right at the crossroads	*Tournez à droite au croisement
Take the second road on the left	*Prenez la deuxième route à gauche
Turn right at the traffic-lights	*Tournez à droite aux feux
Turn left after the bridge	*Tournez à gauche après le pont
The best road is the N.7[1]	*La meilleure route est la N.7
Take the D.21 to . . . and ask again	*Prenez la D.21 jusqu'à . . . et demandez à quelqu'un

---

I. N.7 = *route nationale* 7. All trunk roads are indicated by N followed by a number. D.21 = *route départementale* 21. Secondary roads are indicated by D followed by a number. Motorways are indicated by A followed by a number. A1 = *autoroute* 1 (Paris – Lille).

Motoring

General

Have you a road map, please?	Avez-vous une carte routière, s'il vous plaît?
Where is the nearest car park/ garage?	Où est le parking/le garage le plus proche?
(How long) can I park here?	(Combien de temps) peut-on stationner ici?
May I see your licence/ logbook, please?	*Votre permis de conduire/carte grise, s'il vous plaît
Is this your car?	*C'est votre voiture?
How far is the next petrol station?	À combien d'ici est le prochain poste d'essence?

Car hire

Where can I hire a car?	Où pourrais-je louer une voiture?
I want to hire a car and a driver/a self drive car	Je voudrais louer une voiture avec chauffeur/une voiture sans chauffeur
I need it for two days/a week	J'en ai besoin pour deux jours/une semaine
How much is it to hire it by the hour/day/week?	Combien coûte la location à l'heure/à la journée/à la semaine?
Does that include mileage?	Est-ce que cela comprend le kilométrage?
The charge per kilometre is . . .	*Le tarif du kilomètre est de . . .
Do you want full insurance?	*Voulez-vous une assurance tous risques?
What is the deposit?	Quel est le montant de la caution?
May I see your driving licence?	*Votre permis de conduire, s'il vous plaît
Can I return the car in . . .?	Puis-je ramener la voiture à . . .?
Could you show me the controls/lights, please?	Pourriez-vous me montrer comment fonctionnent les commandes/fonctionne l'éclairage?

Road signs

Allumez vos lanternes	Lights on
Allumez vos phares	Headlights on
Attention	Caution
Attention travaux	Road works ahead
Chaussée déformée	Uneven surface
Chute de pierres	Falling stones
Danger	Danger
Défense de (doubler)	(Overtaking) prohibited
Descente dangereuse/rapide	Steep hill
Déviation	Diversion
Disque (de stationnement) obligatoire	Parking discs required
Douane	Customs
Feux (de circulation)	Traffic lights
Gravillons	Beware flying stones
Passage à niveau	Level crossing
Passage protégé	Priority over traffic from the right
Priorité à droite	Give way to traffic from the right[1]
Prudence	Caution
Roulez lentement	Slow
Route étroite	Narrow road

1. It is important to note that, unless there are road signs to the contrary, vehicles coming from the right have priority at road junctions.

Rue barrée	Road blocked
Rue sans issue	Dead end
Sens interdit	No entry
Sens unique	One way (street)
Serrez à droite	Keep in the righthand lane
Sortie (de camions)	Exit (for lorries)
Stationnement autorisé	Parking allowed
Stationnement interdit	No parking
Stationnement réglementé	Restricted parking
Stop	Stop
Tenez votre droite	Keep right
Toutes directions	Through traffic
Virages	Curves; winding road
Vitesse limite	Maximum speed
Zone bleue	Restricted parking

At the garage or petrol station

Fill it up, please	Le plein, s'il vous plaît
How much is petrol a litre?	Combien vaut le litre d'essence?
. . . litres of standard/premium petrol	. . . litres d'essence ordinaire/de super
. . . francs' worth of four star, please	. . . francs de super, s'il vous plaît

Please check the oil and water	Vérifiez l'huile et l'eau, s'il vous plaît
Could you check the brake/ transmission fluid?	Pouvez-vous vérifier le liquide des freins/le niveau de la boîte?
The oil needs changing	Il faut faire la vidange d'huile
Check the tyre pressures, please	Vérifiez la pression des pneus, s'il vous plaît
Would you clean the windscreen, please?	Pouvez-vous nettoyer le pare-brise, s'il vous plaît?
Please wash the car	Pouvez-vous laver la voiture, s'il vous plaît?
Can I garage the car here?	Est-ce que je peux garer la voiture ici?
What time does the garage close?	À quelle heure ferme le garage?
Where are the toilets?	Où sont les toilettes?

Repairs

My car is broken down	Ma voiture est en panne
May I use your phone?	Puis-je utiliser votre téléphone?
Where is there a . . . agent?	Où y a-t-il une agence . . .?
Have you a breakdown service?	Avez-vous un service de dépannage?
Is there a mechanic?	Y a-t-il un mécanicien?
Can you send someone to look at it/tow it away?	Pouvez-vous envoyer quelqu'un pour l'examiner/pour la remorquer?

It is an automatic and cannot be towed	C'est une automatique et on ne peut pas la remorquer
Where are you?	*Où êtes-vous?
Where is your car?	*Où est votre voiture?
I am on the road from ... to ... near kilometre post ...	Je suis sur la route de ... à ... près de la borne kilométrique ...
How long will you be?	Combien de temps vous faudra-t-il?
I want the car serviced	Veuillez faire les vidanges et un graissage complet, s'il vous plaît
This tyre is flat, can you mend it?	Ce pneu est à plat, pouvez-vous le réparer?
The valve/radiator is leaking	La valve/le radiateur perd
The battery is flat, it needs charging	Ma batterie est déchargée, il faut la recharger
My car won't start	Ma voiture ne démarre pas
It's not running properly	Elle ne marche pas bien
The engine is overheating	Le moteur chauffe
The engine is firing badly/ knocks	Le moteur tourne mal/ cogne
Can you change this faulty plug?	Pouvez-vous remplacer cette bougie défectueuse?
There's a petrol/oil leak	Il y a une fuite d'essence/ d'huile
There's a smell of petrol/ rubber	Il y a une odeur d'essence/de caoutchouc brûlé
There's a rattle/squeak	Il y a un bruit/quelque chose qui grince

Something is wrong with the . . .	Le/la . . . ne marche pas bien
I've got electrical/mechanical trouble	J'ai des ennuis électriques/ mécaniques
The carburettor needs adjusting	Le carburateur a besoin d'un réglage
Can you repair it?	Pouvez-vous réparer cela?
How long will it take to repair?	Combien de temps prendra la réparation?
What will it cost?	Combien est-ce que cela coûtera?
When can I pick the car up?	Quand puis-je venir chercher ma voiture?
I need it as soon as possible/in three hours/in the morning	Je la voudrais le plus tôt possible/ dans trois heures/demain matin
It will take two days	*Cela prendra deux jours
We can repair it temporarily	*Nous pouvons faire une réparation provisoire
We haven't the right spares	*Nous n'avons pas les pièces nécessaires
We have to send for the spares	*Nous devons faire venir les pièces
You will need a new . . .	*Il vous faudra un nouveau (une nouvelle) . . .
Could I have an itemized bill, please?	Pourrais-je avoir une facture détaillée, s'il vous plaît?
I've lost my car key	J'ai perdu ma clé de contact
The lock is broken/jammed	La serrure est cassée/bloquée

Parts of a car

accelerate	accélérer	ak-say-lay-ray
accelerator	l'accélérateur *m*	ak-say-lay-ra-tœr
alternator	l'alternateur *m*	al-tair-na-tœr
antifreeze	l'antigel *m*	ahn-tee-zhel
axle	l'essieu *m*	es-yer
battery	la batterie	ba-tair-ee
bonnet	le capot	ka-poh
boot/trunk	le coffre	koffr
brake	le frein	fran
brake lining	la garniture des freins	gar-nee-tuer day fran
breakdown	la panne	pan
bulb	l'ampoule *f*	ahn-pool
bumper	le pare-choc	par-shok
carburettor	le carburateur	kar-bue-ra-tœr
choke	le starter	star-tair
clutch	l'embrayage *m*	ahn-bray-azh
crankshaft	le vilebrequin	vee-le-bre-kan
cylinder	le cylindre	see-landr
differential gear	le différentiel	dee-fay-rahn-syel
dip stick	la jauge d'huile	zhohzh dweel
distilled water	l'eau distillée	oh dee-stee-lay
distributor	le distributeur	dee-stree-bue-tœr

door	la portière	por-tee-air
door handle	la poignée	pwan-yay
drive (to)	conduire	kohⁿ-dweer
driver	le chauffeur	shoh-fœr
dynamo	la dynamo	dee-na-mo
engine	le moteur	mo-tœr
exhaust	l'échappement *m*	ay-shap-mahⁿ
fan	le ventilateur	vahⁿ-tee-la-tœr
fanbelt	la courroie de ventilateur	koo-rwa
(oil) filter	le filtre (à huile)	feeltr (a weel)
foglamp	le phare antibrouillard	far ahⁿ-tee-brwee-yar
fuse-box	la boîte à fusibles	bwat a fu^e-zeebl
gasket	le joint	zhwaⁿ
gear-box	la boîte de vitesses	bwat de^r vee-tes
gear-lever	le levier du changement de vitesse	le-vee-ay
gears	les vitesses *m*	vee-tes
grease (to)	graisser	gre-say
handbrake	le frein à main	fraⁿ a maⁿ
heater	le chauffage	show-fazh
horn	le klaxon	klak-sohⁿ
ignition	l'allumage *m*	a-lu^e-mazh
ignition key	la clé de contact	klay de kon-takt

indicator (flashing)	le clignotant	kleen-yoh-tah^n
jack	le cric	kreek
lights (headlights)	les phares *m*	far
lock/catch	la serrure	ser-u^{e}r
mirror	le rétroviseur	ray-troh-vee-zœr
number plate	la plaque de police	plak
nut	le boulon	boo-loh^n
oil	l'huile *f*	weel
petrol	l'essence *f*	e-sah^{n}s
petrol can	le bidon d'essence	bee-doh^n
piston	le piston	pee-stoh^n
points	les vis platinées *f*	vee pla-tee-nay
(fuel) pump	la pompe (à essence)	poh^{n}p
puncture	la crevaison	kre^r-vay-zoh^n
radiator	le radiateur	ra-dya-tœr
rear axle	le pont arrière	poh^n a-ree-air
reverse (to)	faire marche arrière	fair marsh a-ree-air
reverse	la marche arrière	marsh a-ree-air
(sliding) roof	le toit (ouvrant)	twa
seat	le siège	see-aizh
shock absorber	l'amortisseur *m*	a-mor-tee-sœr
silencer	le silencieux	see-lah^n-see-e^r
(plug) spanner	la clé (à bougie)	klay

spares	les pièces de rechange *f*	pee-ess der rershahnzh
spare tyre	le pneu de secours	p-ner der se-koor
sparking plug	la bougie	boo-zhee
speed	la vitesse	vee-tes
speedometer	le compteur de vitesse	kohn-tœr
spring	le ressort	re-sor
stall (to)	caler	ka-lay
starter	le démarreur	day-ma-rœr
steering	la direction	dee-rek-syohn
steering wheel	le volant	vo-lahn
suspension	la suspension	suespahn-syohn
tank	le réservoir	ray-zair-vwar
tappets	les culbuteurs *m*	kuel-bue-tœr
transmission	la transmission	trahns-mee-syohn
tyre	le pneu	p-ner
tyre pressure	la pression des pneus	pre-syohn
valve	la soupape	soo-pap
wheel	la roue	roo
window	la vitre/la glace	veetr/glas
windscreen	le pare-brise	par-breeze
windscreen washers	le lave-glace	lav-glas
windscreen wipers	l'essuie-glace *m*	es-we-glas

Accommodation

Booking a room

Rooms to let/vacancies	*Chambres (à louer)
No vacancies	*Complet
Have you a room for the night?	Avez-vous une chambre pour une nuit?
Do you know another good hotel?	Pouvez-vous m'indiquer un autre bon hôtel?
I've reserved a room; my name is . . .	J'ai réservé une chambre; je m'appelle . . .
I want a single room with a shower	Je voudrais une chambre avec douche pour une personne
We want a room with a double bed and a bathroom	Nous voudrions une chambre avec un grand lit et salle de bain(s)
Have you a room with twin beds?	Avez-vous une chambre à deux lits?

How long will you be staying?	*Combien de temps comptez-vous rester?
Is it for one night only?	*C'est pour une nuit seulement?
I want a room for two or three days/for a week/until Friday	Je voudrais une chambre pour deux ou trois jours/pour une semaine/jusqu'à vendredi
What floor is the room on?	À quel étage se trouve la chambre?
Is there a lift/elevator?	Y a-t-il un ascenseur?
Have you a room on the first floor?	Avez-vous une chambre au premier étage?
May I see the room?	Pourrais-je voir la chambre?
I'll take this room	Je prends cette chambre
I don't like this room	Je n'aime pas cette chambre
Have you another one?	En avez-vous une autre?
I want a quiet room	Je veux une chambre calme
There's too much noise	Il y a trop de bruit
I'd like a room with a balcony	Je voudrais une chambre avec balcon
Have you a room looking on to the street/the sea?	Avez-vous une chambre (qui donne) sur la rue/sur la mer?
Is there a telephone/radio/ television in the room?	Y a-t-il le téléphone/la radio/la télévision dans la chambre?
We've only a twin bedded room	*Nous n'avons qu'une chambre à deux lits
This is the only room vacant	*C'est la seule chambre libre

We shall have another room tomorrow	*Nous aurons une autre chambre demain
The room is only available tonight	*Cette chambre n'est libre que ce soir seulement
How much is the room per night?	Quel est le prix de la chambre pour une nuit?
Have you nothing cheaper?	Vous n'avez rien de moins cher?
What do we pay for the children?	Combien devons-nous payer pour les enfants?
Could you put a cot in the room?	Pouvez-vous mettre un petit lit dans la chambre?
Are service and tax included?	Est-ce que le service et la taxe sont compris?
Are meals included?	Est-ce que les repas sont compris?
How much is the room without meals?	Quel est le prix de la chambre sans repas?
How much is full board?	Quel est le prix de la chambre avec pension complète?
I'd like a room with breakfast	Je voudrais une chambre avec petit déjeuner
Do you have a weekly rate?	Avez-vous un tarif hebdomadaire?
Would you fill in the registration form, please?	*Voulez-vous remplir la fiche (de police), s'il vous plaît?
Could I have your passport?	*Puis-je avoir votre passeport?

In your room

Room service	Service dans les chambres
I'd like breakfast in my room, please	Je voudrais prendre le petit déjeuner dans ma chambre, s'il vous plaît
There's no ashtray in my room	Il n'y a pas de cendrier dans ma chambre
Can I have more hangers, please?	Pourrais-je avoir d'autres cintres, s'il vous plaît?
Is there a point for an electric razor?	Est-ce qu'il y a une prise pour rasoir électrique?
What's the voltage?[1]	Quel est le voltage?
Where is the bathroom?	Où est la salle de bains?
Where is the lavatory?	Où sont les toilettes?
Is there a shower?	Y a-t-il des douches?
There are no towels in my room	Il n'y a pas de serviette dans ma chambre
There's no soap	Il n'y a pas de savon
There's no (hot) water	Il n'y a pas d'eau (chaude)
There's no plug in my washbasin	Mon lavabo n'a pas de bouchon
There's no toilet paper in the lavatory	Il n'y a pas de papier hygiénique aux toilettes

1. The voltage in France is 220 volts, but in some places it is still 110 volts. It is therefore important to check it, as it may vary from one place to another.

The lavatory won't flush	La chasse d'eau ne fonctionne pas
May I have the key to the bathroom, please?	Pourrais-je avoir la clé de la salle de bains?
May I have another blanket/ another pillow?	Pourrais-je avoir une autre couverture/un autre oreiller?
These sheets aren't clean	Ces draps ne sont pas propres
I can't open my window, please open it	Je ne peux pas ouvrir ma fenêtre; voulez-vous l'ouvrir, s'il vous plaît
It's too hot/cold	Il fait trop chaud/froid
Can the heating be turned up?	Pouvez-vous chauffer davantage?
Can the heating be turned down?	Pouvez-vous baisser le chauffage?
Is the room air-conditioned?	Est-ce que la chambre est climatisée?
The air conditioning doesn't work	La climatisation ne fonctionne pas
Come in	Entrez
Put it on the table, please	Mettez cela sur la table, s'il vous plaît
I want these shoes cleaned	Je voudrais faire cirer cette paire de chaussures
I want this dress cleaned	Je voudrais faire nettoyer cette robe
I want this suit pressed	Je voudrais faire repasser ce costume
When will it be ready?	Quand est-ce que ce sera prêt?
It will be ready tomorrow	*Ce sera prêt demain

At the porter's desk

My key, please	Ma clé, s'il vous plaît
Have you a map of the town/an amusement guide?	Avez-vous un plan de la ville/un guide des spectacles?
Can I leave this in the safe?	Puis-je déposer ceci dans votre coffre-fort?
Are there any letters for me?	Y a-t-il du courrier pour moi?
Is there any message for me?	Y a-t-il un message pour moi?
If anyone phones, tell them I'll be back at 4.30	Si quelqu'un téléphone, dites que je serai de retour à quatre heures et demie
No one telephoned	*Personne n'a téléphoné
There's a lady/gentleman to see you	*Une dame/un monsieur vous demande
Please ask her/him to come up	Faites la/le monter, s'il vous plaît
I'm coming down	Je descends
Have you any writing paper/ envelopes/stamps?	Avez-vous du papier à lettre/des enveloppes/des timbres?
Please send the chambermaid/ the waiter	Envoyez-moi la femme de chambre/le garçon, s'il vous plaît
I need a guide/an interpreter	J'ai besoin d'un guide/d'un interprète
Where is the dining room?	Où est la salle à manger?

What time is breakfast/lunch/ dinner?	À quelle heure est le petit déjeuner/le déjeuner/le dîner?
Is there a garage?	Est-ce qu'il y a un garage?
Is the hotel open all night?	Est-ce que l'hôtel reste ouvert toute la nuit?
What time does it close?	À quelle heure ferme-t-il?
Please wake me at ...	Veuillez me réveiller à ...

Departure

I have to leave tomorrow	Je dois partir demain
Can we check out at ...?	Pouvons-nous partir à ...?
Can you have my bill ready?	Pouvez-vous préparer ma note?
I shall be coming back on ..., can I book a room for that date?	Je reviendrai le ..., pouvez-vous me réserver une chambre pour cette date?
Could you have my luggage brought down?	Pouvez-vous faire descendre mes bagages?
Please order a taxi for me at ...	Commandez-moi un taxi pour ..., s'il vous plaît
Thank you for a pleasant stay	Je vous remercie de votre aimable accueil

Meeting people

How are you?	Comment allez-vous?
How are things?	Comment ça va?
Fine, thanks; and you?	Très bien, merci; et vous?
May I introduce myself?	Puis-je me présenter?
May I introduce . . .	Permettez que je présente . . .
My name is . . .	Je m'appelle . . .
This is . . .	Je vous présente . . .
Have you met . . . ?	Connaissez-vous . . . ?
Glad to meet you	Heureux de faire votre connaissance
What lovely/awful weather	Quel beau/sale temps!
Isn't is cold/hot today?	Qu'il fait froid/chaud aujourd'hui
Do you think it's going to rain/ snow?	Vous croyez qu'il va pleuvoir/ neiger?
Will it be sunny tomorrow?	Est-ce qu'il fera beau demain?
Am I disturbing you?	Est-ce que je vous dérange?

Go away	Allez-vous en/Partez
Leave me alone	Laissez-moi tranquille
Sorry to have troubled you	Excusez-moi de vous avoir dérangé
Do you live/are you staying here?	Vous habitez/Vous séjournez ici?
Is this your first time here?	C'est la première fois que vous venez ici?
Do you like it here?	Vous vous plaisez ici?
Are you on your own?	Vous êtes seul(e)?
I am with my family/parents/ a friend	Je suis avec ma famille/mes parents/un ami, une amie.
Where do you come from?	D'où venez-vous?
I come from . . .	Je viens de . . .
What do you do?	Qu'est-ce que vous faites dans la vie?
What are you studying?	Qu'est-ce que vous étudiez?
I'm on holiday/ a (business) trip	Je suis en vacances/en voyage (d'affaires)
Would you like a cigarette?	Voulez-vous une cigarette?
Try one of mine	Essayez une des miennes
They're very mild/rather strong	Elles sont très douces/plutôt fortes
Do you have a light, please?	Avez-vous du feu, s'il vous plaît?
Do you smoke?	Vous fumez?
No, I don't, thanks	Non merci

I have given it up	J'ai cessé de fumer
Help yourself	Servez-vous
Can I get you a drink/another drink?	Puis je vous offrir un verre/un autre verre?
I'd like a . . . please	Je prendrai un . . . s'il vous plaît
No thanks, I'm all right	Non merci, ça va

Going out

Are you waiting for someone?	Vous attendez quelqu'un?
Are you doing anything tonight/tomorrow afternoon?	Qu'est-ce que vous faites ce soir/demain après-midi?
Could we have coffee/a drink somewhere?	Est-ce qu'on pourrait aller prendre un café/un verre quelque part?
Would you go out with me?	Voulez-vous sortir avec moi?
Shall we go to the cinema/theatre/beach?	On va au cinéma/au théâtre/à la plage?
Would you like to go dancing/for a drive?	Voulez-vous aller danser/faire une promenade en voiture?
Do you know a good disco/restaurant?	Connaissez-vous une bonne discothèque/un bon restaurant?
Can you come to dinner/for a drink?	Pouvez-vous venir dîner/prendre un verre?

We're giving/there is a party; would you like to come?	Nous organisons/il y a une 'party'; voulez-vous venir?
Can I bring a (girl) friend?	Puis-je amener un ami/une amie?
Thanks for the invitation	Merci de l'invitation
Where shall we meet?	Où nous retrouverons-nous?
What time shall I/we come?	À quelle heure dois-je/ devons-nous venir?
I could pick you up at (*place/time*)	Je pourrais passer vous prendre à...
Could you meet me at (*time*) outside (*place*)?	Pouvez-vous me rejoindre à... devant...?
What time do you have to be back?	À quelle heure devez-vous être de retour?
May I see you home?	Puis-je vous raccompagner chez vous?
Can we give you a lift home/to your hotel?	Pouvons-nous vous reconduire chez vous/à votre hôtel?
Can I see you again?	Est-ce qu'on peut se revoir?
Where do you live?	Où habitez-vous?
What is your telephone number?	Quel est votre numéro de téléphone?
Do you live alone?	Vous vivez seul(e)?
Thanks for the evening/drink/ ride	Merci pour la soirée/le pot/la promenade
It was lovely	C'était très sympathique

It's been nice talking to you	J'ai eu beaucoup de plaisir à vous parler
Hope to see you again soon	J'espère vous revoir bientôt
See you soon/later/tomorrow	À bientôt/à plus tard/à demain

Restaurant

Going to a restaurant

Can you suggest a good restaurant/a cheap restaurant/a vegetarian restaurant?

Connaissez-vous un bon restaurant/un restaurant bon marché/un restaurant végétarien?

I'd like to book a table for four at 1 p.m.

Je voudrais réserver une table pour quatre pour une heure

I've reserved a table; my name is...

J'ai réservé un table; je m'appelle...

We did not make a reservation

Nous n'avons pas réservé de table

Have you a table for three?

Avez-vous une table pour trois?

Is there a table on the terrace/by the window/in a corner?

Y a-t-il une table à la terrasse/près de la fenêtre/dans un coin?

This way, please

*Par ici, s'il vous plaît

We shall have a table free in half an hour

*Il y aura une table libre dans une demi-heure

You would have to wait about . . . minutes	*Vous devez attendre environ . . . minutes
We don't serve lunch until 12	*On ne sert pas le déjeuner avant midi
We don't serve dinner until 8 p.m.	*On ne sert pas le dîner avant huit heures
We stop serving at 11 o'clock	*On ne sert plus après onze heures
Where is the cloakroom?	Où sont les toilettes?
It is downstairs	*Elles sont en bas
We are in a hurry	Nous sommes pressés
Do you serve snacks?	Est-ce que vous servez des casse-croûte?

Ordering

Service charge	*Supplément pour le service
Service and V.A.T. (not) included	*Service et T.V.A. (non) compris
Waiter/waitress (*address*)	Garçon/mademoiselle
May I see the menu/the wine list, please?	Pourrais-je voir le menu/la carte des vins, s'il vous plaît?
Is there a set menu?	Y a-t-il un menu à prix fixe?
I want something light	Je voudrais quelque chose de léger
Do you have children's helpings?	Avez-vous de petites portions pour les enfants?

What is your dish of the day?	Quel est le plat du jour?
What do you recommend?	Qu'est-ce que vous recommandez?
Can you tell me what this is?	Pouvez-vous me dire ce que c'est?
What is the speciality of the restaurant/of the region?	Quelle est la spécialité de ce restaurant/du pays?
Would you like to try ...?	*Voulez-vous goûter ...?
There's no more ...	*Il n'y a plus de ...
I'd like ...	Je voudrais ...
May I have peas instead of beans?	Pourrais-je avoir des petits pois à la place des haricots?
Is it hot or cold?	Est-ce chaud ou froid?
Where are our drinks?	Où sont nos boissons?
Why is the food taking so long?	Pourquoi est-ce que le service est si lent?
This isn't what I ordered, I want ...	Ce n'est pas ce que j'ai commandé, je veux ...
Without oil/sauce, please	Sans huile/sauce, s'il vous plaît
Some more bread, please	Un peu plus de pain, s'il vous plaît
A little more ...	Un peu plus de ...
This is bad	Ce n'est pas bon
This is uncooked	Ce n'est pas cuit
This is overcooked	C'est trop cuit
This bread is stale	Ce pain est rassis

This is too cold/salty

C'est trop froid/salé

This plate/spoon (knife/glass) is not clean

Cette assiette/cuiller (ce couteau/verre) n'est pas propre

Paying

The bill, please

L'addition, s'il vous plaît

Does it include service?

Est-ce que le service est compris?

Please check the bill – I don't think it's correct

Voulez-vous vérifier l'addition; je crois qu'il y a une erreur

What is this amount for?

À quoi correspond cette somme?

I didn't have soup

Je n'ai pas pris de soupe

I had an entrecôte, not a tournedos

J'ai pris une entrecôte, pas un tournedos

May we have separate bills?

Pouvez-vous faire l'addition séparément?

Do you take credit cards/traveller's cheques?

Acceptez-vous les cartes de crédit/les chèques de voyage?

Keep the change

Gardez la monnaie

Breakfast and tea

Breakfast[1]	Le petit déjeuner
A large white/black coffee, please	Un grand café crème/noir, s'il vous plaît
A cup of tea/chocolate, please	Une tasse de thé/chocolat, s'il vous plaît
I'd like tea with milk/lemon	Je voudrais du thé au lait/au citron
May we have some sugar, please?	Pourriez-vous nous donner du sucre, s'il vous plaît?
A roll/bread/toast and butter	Un petit pain/du pain/du pain grillé avec du beurre
Croissants (crescent-shaped rolls)	Des croissants
More butter, please	Un peu plus de beurre, s'il vous plaît
Have you some jam/marmalade?	Avez-vous de la confiture/de la confiture d'orange?
I would like a boiled egg	Je voudrais un œuf à la coque
Bacon/ham and eggs, please	Des œufs au bacon/au jambon, s'il vous plaît
Cheese	Le fromage
What fruit juices have you?	Quelles sortes de jus de fruit avez-vous?

1. *Le petit déjeuner* (*complet*) usually consists of coffee, tea or chocolate, rolls, croissants and butter. It is normally the only meal taken in a café.

Orange/grapefruit/tomato juice	Le jus d'orange/de pamplemousse /de tomate
Yoghurt	Le yaourt
Cereal	Les céréales *f*
Pastry	La pâtisserie
Cake	Le gâteau

Snacks and picnics

Can I have a . . . sandwich, please?	Puis-je avoir un sandwich au . . ., s'il vous plaît?
What are those things over there?	Qu'est-ce que c'est que ça là-bas?
What are they made of?	Avec quoi est-ce fait?
What is in them?	Qu'est-ce qu'il y a dedans?
I'll have one of those, please	J'en prendrai un de ceux-là

Biscuits	les biscuits *m*
Bread	le pain
Butter	le beurre
Cheese	le fromage
Chips	les frites *f*
Chocolate bar	la tablette de chocolat
Eggs	les œufs *m*
Ham	le jambon

Hamburger	le hamburger
Ice cream (*flavours* p. 98)	la glace
Pancakes	les crèpes *f*
Pickles	les conserves au vinaigre *f*
Roll	le petit pain
Salad	la salade
Sausage	la saucisse
Sausage roll	le friand
Snack	le casse-croûte
Snack bar	le snack bar
Soup	la soupe
Tomato	la tomate
Waffles	les gaufres *f*

Drinks[1]

Bar	Le bar/la buvette
Café, pub	Le café
Tea room	Le salon de thé
What will you have to drink?	*Que désirez-vous comme boisson?
A bottle of the local wine, please	Une bouteille de vin du pays, s'il vous plaît

1. For the names of beverages see p. 99.

Do you serve wine by the glass?	Est-ce que vous servez du vin au verre?
Carafe/glass	La carafe/le verre
Bottle/half bottle	La bouteille/demi-bouteille
Two glasses of beer, please	Deux demis, s'il vous plaît
Large/small beer	Un sérieux/un demi
Light/dark beer	La bière blonde/brune
Do you have draught beer?	Avez-vous de la bière à la pression?
Two more beers, please	Encore deux demis, s'il vous plaît
Neat	Pur
On the rocks	Avec de la glace
With water/soda water	Avec de l'eau/du soda
Mineral water (with/without gas)	L'eau minérale (gazeuse/non gazeuse)
Ice cubes	Les glaçons *m*
Cheers!	À votre santé
I'd like another glass of water, please	Je voudrais encore un verre d'eau, s'il vous plaît
The same again, please	La même chose, s'il vous plaît
Three black coffees and one white	Trois cafés noirs et un café-crème
Tea with milk/lemon	Le thé au lait/au citron
May we have an ashtray?	Pouvez-vous nous donner un cendrier?

Restaurant vocabulary

ashtray	le cendrier	sah^n-dree-ay
bill	l'addition f	la-dee-syoh^n
bowl	le bol	bol
bread	le pain	pa^n
butter	le beurre	bœr
cloakroom	les toilettes f/le lavabo	twa-let/la-va-bo
course (dish)	le plat	pla
cream	la crème	kraim
cup	la tasse	tas
fork	la fourchette	foor-shet
glass	le verre	vair
headwaiter	le maître d'hôtel	metr do-tel
hungry (to be)	(avoir) faim	av-war fa^n
knife	le couteau	koo-toh
matches	les allumettes f	a-lu^{e}met
menu	le menu	me^r-nu^e
mustard	la moutarde	moo-tard
napkin	la serviette	sair-vyet
oil	l'huile f	lweel
pepper	le poivre	pwavr
plate	l'assiette f	las-yet
restaurant	le restaurant	res-tor-ah^n

salt	le sel	sel
sauce	la sauce	sohs
saucer	la soucoupe	soo-koop
service	le service	sair-vees
spoon	la cuiller	kwee-yay
sugar	le sucre	su^{e}kr
table	la table	tabl
table-cloth	la nappe	nap
thirsty (to be)	(avoir) soif	av-war swaf
tip	le pourboire	poor-bwar
toothpick	le cure-dent	ku^{e}r-dah^n
vegetarian	végétarien	vay-zhay-ta-rya^n
vinegar	le vinaigre	vee-negr
waiter	le garçon	gar-soh^n
waitress	la serveuse	sair-vœz
water	l'eau *f*	loh

The menu

HORS D'ŒUVRES

Anchois

Artichaut

Asperges

HORS D'ŒUVRES

anchovy

artichoke

asparagus

Assiette anglaise	assorted cold cuts
Cœurs d'artichaut	artichoke hearts
Cœurs de palmier	palm hearts
Confit d'oie	preserved goose
Coquilles St Jacques	scallops
Cornichons	gherkins
Crudités	salad vegetables (tomatoes, beetroot, carrot, cucumber, etc.) with vinaigrette dressing
Escargots	snails
Foie gras truffé	goose liver pâté with truffles
Grenouilles	frogs (legs)
Huîtres	oysters
Jambon	ham
Melon	melon
Moules marinières	mussels in white wine sauce
Œuf dur mayonnaise	egg mayonnaise
Pâté (de campagne)	pâté
Pipérade	tomatoes and peppers cooked with scrambled egg
Quiche lorraine	a tart with a filling of egg custard, bacon, onions and cheese
Rillettes	a kind of potted pork, or goose and pork
Salade niçoise	mixed salad with tuna and anchovies

Saucisson	sausage (salami type)
Tarte à l'oignon	onion tart
Terrine (de lapin/canard)	a kind of pâté (rabbit/duck)

SOUPES/POTAGES	SOUPS
Bisque (de homard)	a rich soup made from shellfish (lobster)
Bouillabaisse	a substantial soup made from different kinds of fish
Consommé	a clear strong beef soup
Crème/velouté d'asperges/de tomates	cream of asparagus/tomato soup
Crème vichyssoise	a cold soup made with chicken stock, leeks and cream
Petite marmite	a substantial clear soup with a predominant flavour of chicken
Potage aux champignons	mushroom soup
Potage julienne	clear soup with finely shredded vegetables
Potage parmentier	potato soup
Potage au poulet	chicken soup
Potage Saint-Germain	pea soup
Potage aux tomates	tomato soup
Soupe aux choux	cabbage soup
Soupe de légumes	vegetable soup

Soupe à l'oignon gratinée	onion soup poured over slices of bread covered with grated cheese
Soupe de poisson	fish soup
Soupe du jour	soup of the day

POISSON	FISH
Anguille	eel
Barbue	brill
Brochet	pike
Calmar	squid
Carpe	carp
Colin	hake
Crabe	crab
Crevettes	shrimps/prawns
Dorade	sea bream
Écrevisses	(freshwater) crayfish
Fruits de mer	shellfish
Hareng	herring
Homard	lobster
Huîtres	oysters
Langouste	rock lobster
Langoustines	Dublin Bay prawns/scampi
Lotte	angler-fish, monkfish

Loup de mer	sea bass
Maquereau	mackerel
Merlan	whiting
Merluche	hake
Morue (sèche)	(dried) cod
Moules	mussels
Mulet	grey mullet
Oursin	sea urchin
Palourdes	clams
Plie	plaice
Poulpe	octopus
Praires	oyster-like shellfish
Quenelle (de brochet)	a fish (pike) dumpling
Raie	skate
Rouget	red mullet
Sardines	sardines
Saumon	salmon
Sole	sole
Thon	tunny
Truite	trout
Turbot	turbot

VIANDE	MEAT
Bœuf:	*beef:*
Bifteck	steak
Bœuf bourguignon	beef cooked in red wine with mushrooms and onions
Bœuf en daube	beef braised in red wine and well seasoned with herbs
Carbonnade de bœuf	a rich beef stew made with beer
Châteaubriand	steak taken from the heart of a fillet of beef
Côte/entrecôte	T-bone/rib steak
Filet/contre-filet	fillet/loin steak
Pot-au-feu	beef stewed with root vegetables
Rôti	roast
Tournedos	a thick steak cut from the eye of the fillet
Agneau/mouton:	*lamb/mutton:*
Carré d'agneau	loin of lamb with herbs
Côtelette	chop
Épaule	shoulder
Gigot	leg
Veau:	*veal:*
Côtelette	cutlet
Escalope	escalope

Longe	loin
Médaillon	slice cut from the loin
Poitrine	breast
Tête de veau vinaigrette	calf's head with vinaigrette sauce

Porc:	*pork:*
Basse-côtes	spare ribs
Charcuterie	assorted preserved pork products
Cochon de lait	sucking pig
Côte	chop
Longe	loin
Pieds	trotters

Andouilles/andouillettes	sausages made of chitterlings, usually grilled
Bacon	bacon
Boudin	black pudding or blood sausage, fried or grilled
Boulettes	meatballs/rissoles
Cassoulet	casserole of pork, sausage and beans, with preserved goose
Cervelle	brains
Choucroute garnie	sauerkraut with pork, ham, sausage, and boiled potatoes
Crépinettes	small flat sausages flavoured with herbs and brandy

Foie	liver
Jambon au madère	ham in madeira sauce
Langue	tongue
Ragoût	stew
Ris de veau	sweetbreads
Rognons	kidneys
Saucisses de Francfort/de Strasbourg	Frankfurters
Saucisses de Toulouse	big sausages with thickly cut forcemeat, grilled or fried
Tripes à la mode de Caen	tripe cooked with onions and carrots

VOLAILLE ET GIBIER	POULTRY AND GAME
Aile	wing
Blanc	breast
Caille	quail
Canard	duck
Canard à l'orange	duck with orange sauce
Canard aux olives	duck with olives
Chevreuil	venison
Civet de lièvre	jugged hare
Coq au vin	chicken cooked in red wine with bacon, mushrooms, and onions
Cuisse	leg

Dinde	turkey
Faisan	pheasant
Lapin	rabbit
Lièvre	hare
Oie	goose
Perdreau, perdrix	partridge
Pigeon	pigeon
Pintade	guinea fowl
Poule-au-pot	chicken stewed with root vegetables
Poulet	chicken
Poussin	spring chicken
Sanglier	wild boar
Suprême	breast

LÉGUMES/SALADES	VEGETABLES/SALADS
Ail	garlic
Artichaut	artichoke
Asperges	asparagus
Aubergine	aubergine/eggplant
Betterave	beetroot
Carotte	carrot
Céleri	celery
Champignon (cèpe/morille/chanterelle)	mushroom

Chicorée	endive/chicory
Chou	cabbage
Choucroute	sauerkraut
Choux de Bruxelles	Brussels sprouts
Chou-fleur	cauliflower
Concombre	cucumber
Courgette	baby marrow/zucchini
Endive	chicory
Épinards	spinach
Fenouil	fennel
Fèves	broad beans
Flageolets	green kidney beans
Haricots verts	green beans
Laitue	lettuce
Lentilles	lentils
Maïs	sweet corn
Marrons	chestnuts
Navet	turnip
Oignon	onion
Petits pois	peas
Piment	pepper
Poireau	leek
Pommes de terre	potatoes
allumettes	chips

chips	crisps
frites	chips/French fries
en purée	creamed
Ratatouille	casseroled onion, aubergine, tomato, pepper and courgette
Riz	rice
Salade (verte)	salad (even without *verte* it usually means a green salad)
Salade variée/mélangée	mixed salad
Tomate	tomato

ŒUFS — EGGS

À la coque	boiled
Brouillés	scrambled
Omelette (nature/aux fines herbes/aux champignons)	omelette (plain/with herbs/with mushrooms)
Pochés	poached
Soufflé	soufflé
Sur le plat	fried

FROMAGE — CHEESE

Bresse bleu	soft blue cheese
Brie	soft cheese made in large thin wheels
Camembert	another unpressed soft cheese, made in smaller rounds

Cantal	hard and yellow cheese from mountain pastures
Chèvre	any cheese made of goats' milk
Emmenthal	hard-pressed Swiss cheese with large holes
Gruyère	hard-pressed Swiss cheese, saltier and with smaller holes than Emmenthal
Munster	small semi-hard cheese with a powerful aroma
Pont l'éveque	soft cheese made of unskimmed milk, the more pungent the older it becomes
Port Salut	medium-hard and of medium taste, this is France's great all-purpose cheese
Roquefort	semi-hard blue cheese made of ewes' milk
Saint Paulin	mild semi-soft cheese, much like Port Salut
Croque-monsieur	toasted ham and cheese sandwich
Fondue	hot dip of cheese and white wine, eaten with chunks of bread on long forks
Raclette	grilled cheese, eaten with potatoes and pickles

DESSERTS	DESSERTS
Beignets	fritters
Coupe glacée	ice cream sundae
Crème caramel	caramel pudding
Crêpes	pancakes
Crêpes Suzette	thin pancakes flamed with brandy and orange liqueur
Gâteau	cake

Glaces	ices
à la vanille	vanilla
au café	coffee
au chocolat	chocolate
Granités	water ices
Omelette au rhum	rum omelette
Omelette norvégienne	baked Alaska
Salade de fruits	fruit salad
Soufflé au Grand Marnier	soufflé flavoured with orange liqueur
Tarte (aux pommes)	(apple) tart

FRUITS ET NOIX   FRUIT AND NUTS

Abricot	apricot
Amande	almond
Ananas	pineapple
Banane	banana
Cerise	cherry
Citron	lemon
Figue	fig
Fraises (des bois)	(wild) strawberries
Framboise	raspberry
Groseille	red currant
Groseille à maquereau	gooseberry
Marron	chestnut

Melon	melon
Mûre	blackberry/mulberry
Noisette	hazelnut
Noix	walnut
Orange	orange
Pamplemousse	grapefruit
Pastèque	water melon
Pêche	peach
Poire	pear
Pomme	apple
Prune	plum
Raisin	grape
Raisin sec	raisin
Reine-claude	greengage

BOISSONS	DRINKS
Bière	beer
blonde	lager
brune	(brown) ale
Champagne	champagne
Cidre	cider
Cognac	cognac/brandy
Eau minérale	mineral water
Jus de fruit	fruit juice

Limonade	lemonade
Orangeade	orangeade
Porto	port
Rhum	rum
Vin	wine
blanc	white
rosé	rosé
rouge	red
doux	sweet
sec	dry
pétillant/mousseux	sparkling
Vin de Xérès	sherry

SOME COOKING METHODS

à la broche	barbecued
à l'étuvée	steamed
au beurre/à l'huile	with butter/oil
au four	baked
bouilli	boiled
braisé	braised
chaud/froid	hot/cold
cru	raw
en cocotte	casseroled
en gelée	in aspic
en purée	puréed/creamed

farci	stuffed
frit	fried
fumé	smoked
grillé	grilled
mariné	marinated
mijoté/en ragoût	stewed
persillé	with parsley
poché	poached
râpé	grated
rôti	roast
viande – saignant	meat – rare
à point	medium
bien cuit	well-done

SAUCES

aïoli	garlic mayonnaise
à l'américaine	cooked in white wine with brandy, tomatoes and onions
béarnaise	creamy sauce flavoured with shallots and tarragon
béchamel	white sauce
bigarrade	with orange
bordelaise	mushrooms, shallots and red wine
bourguignonne	red wine and herbs
Café de Paris	butter with brandy and herbs
chasseur	(red) wine, mushrooms, shallots and herbs

financière	madeira, olives and mushrooms
fines herbes	with herbs
florentine	with spinach
hollandaise	mayonnaise
lyonnaise	with onions
maître d'hôtel	butter, parsley and lemon juice
marchand de vin	red wine and shallots
marinière	white wine, own broth and egg yolk
meunière	brown butter, parsley and lemon juice
mornay	with cheese sauce
normande	cream with mushrooms and egg
parmentier	with potatoes
provençale	onions, tomatoes and garlic
rémoulade	mustard-flavoured mayonnaise
soubise	onion sauce
thermidor	cream sauce
vinaigrette	oil and vinegar dressing

Shopping[1] and services

Where to go

Which is the best . . . ?	Quel est le meilleur/la meilleure
Where is the nearest . . . ?	Quel est le/la . . . le/la plus proche?
Can you recommend a . . . ?	Pouvez-vous me recommander un/une . . . ?
Where is the market?	Où est le marché?
Is there a market every day?	Est-ce qu'il y a un marché tous les jours?
Where can I buy . . . ?	Où puis-je acheter . . . ?
When are the shops open?	Quand est-ce que les magasins sont ouverts?

antique shop	le magasin d'antiquités	ma-ga-za^n dah^n-tee-kee-tay
baker	la boulangerie	boo-lah^n-zhe^r-ree

[1]. Most smaller shops are open by 8.30; they close for lunch and stay open until 7 or 8 in the evening.

barber (see p. 115)	le coiffeur	kwa-fœr
bookshop	la librairie	lee-brair-ee
butcher (see p. 91)	la boucherie/charcuterie	boo-sher-ree/shar-kue-ter-ree
cake shop	la pâtisserie	pa-tee-ser-ree
chemist (see p. 110)	la pharmacie	far-ma-see
confectioner	la confiserie	kohn-fee-ser-ree
dairy	la crémerie	kre-mer-ree
department store (see pp. 105 ff.)	le grand magasin	grahn ma-ga-zan
dry cleaner (see p. 118)	la teinturerie	tan-tue-rer-ree
fishmonger (see p. 89)	la poissonnerie	pwa-son-er-ree
florist	le fleuriste	flœr-eest
greengrocer (see pp. 94 and 98)	le marchand de légumes	mar-shahn de lay-guem
grocer (see p. 114)	l'épicier m	lay-pee-syay
hairdresser (see p. 115)	le coiffeur	kwa-fœr
hardware store (see p. 117)	la quincaillerie	kain-kah-yer-ree
jeweller	le bijoutier	bee-zhoo-tyay
launderette	la laverie (automatique)	lah-ver-ree oh-toh-mah-teek
laundry (see p. 118)	la blanchisserie	blahn-shee-ser-ree
liquor/wine store (see p. 99)	le marchand de vins	mar-shahn de van

newsagent	le marchand de journaux	mar-shah^n de zhoor-noh
optician	l'opticien m	lop-tee-sya^n
shoe shop (see p. 112)	le magasin de chaussures	ma-ga-za^n de shoh-su^{e}r
shoemaker	le cordonnier	kor-do-nyay
stationer	la papeterie	pa-pe-tree
supermarket	le supermarché	su^e-pair-mar-shay
tobacconist (see p. 121)	le bureau de tabac	bu^e-roh de ta-bak
toy shop	le magasin de jouets	ma-ga-za^n de zhoo-ay

In the shop

Self service	*Libre-service/self-service
Sale (clearance)	*Soldes
Cash desk	*Caisse
Shop assistant	Le vendeur/la vendeuse
Manager	Le directeur/le gérant
Can I help you?	*Vous désirez?
I want to buy ...	Je voudrais ...
Do you sell ...?	Est-ce que vous avez ...?
I'm just looking round	Je jette un coup d'œil/je regarde

I don't want to buy anything now	Je ne veux rien acheter maintenant
Could you show me . . . ?	Pouvez-vous me montrer . . . ?
We do not have that	*Nous n'avons pas ça
You'll find them at that counter	*Vous trouverez cela à ce rayon
We've sold out but we'll have more tomorrow	*Nous n'en avons plus, mais nous en aurons d'autres demain
Anything else?	*Vous faut-il autre chose?
That will be all	Ce sera tout
Will you take it with you?	*C'est pour emporter?
I'll take it with me	Je l'emporte
Please send them to this address/X hotel	Envoyez-les à cette adresse/ à l'hôtel X

Choosing

I want something in leather/ green	Je veux quelque chose en cuir/en vert
I need it to match this	Je veux quelque chose qui aille avec ceci
I like the one in the window	J'aime celui/celle qui est en vitrine
Could I see that one?	Puis-je voir celui-là/celle-là?
I like the colour but not the style	J'aime la couleur mais pas le genre

I want a darker/lighter shade	Je veux une teinte plus foncée/plus claire
I need something warmer/thinner	Je veux quelque chose de plus chaud/de plus léger
Do you have one in another colour/size?	En avez-vous un(e) dans une autre couleur/taille?
Have you anything better/cheaper?	Avez-vous quelque chose de mieux/de meilleur marché?
How much is this?	Combien coûte ceci?
That is too much for me	C'est trop cher pour moi
What's it made of?	En quoi est-ce?
What size is this?[1]	C'est quelle taille/pointure?
I take size . . .	Je prends du . . .
The English/American size is . . .	En Angleterre/en Amérique c'est du . . .
My chest/waist measurement is . . .	Je fais . . . de tour de poitrine/de taille
Can I try it on?	Puis-je l'essayer?
It's too short/long/tight/loose	C'est trop court/long/serré/ample
Have you a larger/smaller one?	Avez-vous plus grand/plus petit?

1. Size = *taille* except for shoes, gloves and hats, when *pointure* should be used. See table (p. 113) for continental sizes.

Colours

beige	beige	bezh
black	noir	nwar
blue	bleu	ble^r
brown	brun/marron	bre^n/ma-roh^n
gold	doré	do-ray
green	vert	vair
grey	gris	gree
mauve	mauve	mohv
orange	orange	orah^{n}zh
pink	rose	roz
purple	violet	vee-o-lay
red	rouge	roozh
silver	argent	ar-zhah^n
white	blanc	blah^n
yellow	jaune	zhohn

Complaints

I want to see the manager	Je veux voir le patron/le gérant
I bought this yesterday	J'ai acheté ceci hier
It doesn't work	Cela ne marche pas
It doesn't fit	Ça ne va pas

This is dirty/stained/torn/ broken/cracked/bad

C'est sale/taché/déchiré/ cassé/fêlé/mauvais

Will you change it, please?

Pouvez-vous me le changer?

Will you refund my money?

Pouvez-vous me rembourser?

Here is the receipt

Voici le reçu

Paying

How much is this?

Combien coûte ceci?

That's 50 F, please

*Cela fait cinquante francs

They are one franc each

*Ils/elles coûtent un franc pièce

How much does that come to?

Combien est-ce que cela fait?

That will be ...

*Cela fait ...

Will you take English/ American currency?

Acceptez-vous l'argent anglais/ les dollars?

Do you take credit cards/ traveller's cheques?

Acceptez-vous les cartes de crédit/les chèques de voyage?

Please pay the cashier

*Payez à la caisse, s'il vous plaît

May I have a receipt, please?

Pourriez-vous me donner un reçu?

You've given me the wrong change

Vous vous êtes trompé en me rendant la monnaie

Chemist

Can you prepare this prescription for me, please?	Pouvez-vous me préparer cette ordonnance, s'il vous plaît?
Have you a small first aid kit?	Avez-vous une petite trousse de secours?
I want some aspirin/sun cream for children	Je voudrais de l'aspirine/de la crème solaire pour enfants
A tin of adhesive plaster	Une boîte de sparadrap
Can you suggest something for indigestion/constipation/diarrhoea?	Pouvez-vous me recommander quelque chose pour le mal d'estomac/pour la constipation/pour la diarrhée?
I want something for insect bites	Je voudrais quelque chose contre les piqûres d'insectes
Can you give me something for sunburn?	Pouvez-vous me donner quelque chose pour les coups de soleil?
I want some throat lozenges/antiseptic cream	Je voudrais des pastilles pour la gorge/une crème antiseptique
Do you have sanitary towels/tampons/cotton wool?	Avez-vous des serviettes hygiéniques/des tampons hygiéniques/de la ouate?
I need something for insect bites/a hangover/travel sickness	Je voudrais quelque chose pour les piqûres d'insectes/les excès de boisson/le mal des transports

Toilet requisites

A packet of razor blades, please	Un paquet de lames de rasoir, s'il vous plaît
How much is this after-shave lotion?	Combien coûte cette lotion après-rasage?
A tube of toothpaste, please	Un tube de pâte dentifrice, s'il vous plaît
A box of paper handkerchiefs, please	Une boîte de mouchoirs en papier, s'il vous plaît
A roll of toilet paper	Un rouleau de papier hygiénique
I want some eau-de-cologne/perfume	Je voudrais de l'eau-de-cologne/du parfum
May I try it?	Puis-je l'essayer?
What kinds of toilet soap have you?	Quelles marques de savonnettes avez-vous?
A bottle/tube of shampoo, please, for dry/greasy hair	Un flacon/un tube de shampooing pour cheveux secs/gras
Do you have any suntan oil/cream?	Avez-vous de l'huile/de la crème solaire?

Clothes and shoes[1]

I want a hat/sunhat	Je voudrais un chapeau/un chapeau de paille
May I see some dresses, please?	Pourrais-je voir des robes, s'il vous plaît?
Where is the underwear/ haberdashery/coats department?	Où se trouve le rayon de la lingerie/ de la mercerie/des manteaux?
Where are beach clothes?	Où sont les vêtements pour la plage?
The fashion department is on the second floor	*Le rayon des modes est au deuxième étage
I want a short/long sleeved shirt	Je voudrais une chemise à manches courtes/longues
Where can I find socks/ stockings/tights?	Où pourrais-je trouver des chaussettes/des bas/un collant?
I am looking for a blouse/bra/ dress/jumper	Je cherche un chemisier/un soutien-gorge/une robe/un chandail
I need a coat/raincoat/jacket	Je voudrais un manteau/un imperméable/une veste
Do you sell buttons/elastic/zips?	Est-ce que vous vendez des boutons/de l'élastique/des fermetures éclair?
I need a pair of walking shoes	Je voudrais une paire de chaussures pour la marche

1. For sizes see p. 113.

I need a pair of beach sandals/ black shoes	Je désire une paire de sandales pour la plage/de chaussures noires
These heels are too high/too low	Ces talons sont trop hauts/trop courts

Clothing sizes

WOMEN'S DRESSES, ETC.

British	32	34	36	38	40	42	44
American	10	12	14	16	18	20	22
French	38	40	42	44	46	48	50

MEN'S SUITS

British and American	36	38	40	42	44	46
Continental	46	48	50	52	54	56

MEN'S SHIRTS

British and American	14	14½	15	15½	16	16½	17
Continental	36	37	38	39	41	42	43

STOCKINGS

British and American	8	8½	9	9½	10	10½	11
Continental	0	1	2	3	4	5	6

SOCKS

British and American	9½	10	10½	11	11½
Continental	38–39	39–40	40–41	41–42	42–43

SHOES

British	1	2	3	4	5	6	7	8	9	10
American	2½	3½	4½	5½	6½	7½	8½	9½	10½	11½
Continental	33	34–35	36	37	38	39–40	41	42	43	44

British	11	12
American	12½	13½
Continental	45	46

Food[1]

Give me a kilo/half a kilo (pound) of . . ., please	Donnez-moi un kilo/un demi-kilo (une livre) de . . ., s'il vous plaît
100 grammes of sweets/ chocolate, please	Cent grammes de bonbons/de chocolat, s'il vous plaît
A bottle of milk/wine/beer, please	Une bouteille de lait/vin/bière, s'il vous plaît
Is there anything back on the bottle?	Est-ce que la bouteille est consignée?
I want a jar/tin/can/packet of . . .	Je voudrais un pot/une boîte/ un paquet de . . .

1. See also the various MENU sections (p. 86ff.) and WEIGHTS AND MEASURES (p. 166).

Do you sell frozen foods?	Vendez-vous des aliments surgelés?
These pears are too hard/soft	Ces poires sont trop dures/molles
Is it fresh?	Est-ce frais?
Are they ripe?	Sont-ils mûrs?
This is bad	C'est mauvais
This is stale	Ce n'est pas frais
A loaf of bread, please[1]	Un pain, s'il vous plaît
How much a kilo/bottle?	Combien est-ce le kilo/la bouteille?

Hairdresser and barber

May I make an appointment for this morning/tomorrow afternoon?	Pourrais-je prendre un rendez-vous pour ce matin/pour demain après-midi?
What time?	À quelle heure?
I want my hair cut	Je voudrais me faire couper les cheveux
Just a trim, please	Simplement rafraîchir, s'il vous plaît

1. French loaves:
    une flute – a small thin stick.
    une baguette – a longer, slightly thicker stick (the most common French bread).
    un bâtard – shorter and thicker than a *baguette*.
    un pain de mie – English loaf.

Not too short at the sides	Pas trop courts sur le côté
I'll have it shorter at the back, please	Je les voudrais un peu plus courts derrière, s'il vous plaît
My hair is oily/dry	Mes cheveux sont gras/secs
I want a shampoo	Je voudrais un shampooing
I want my hair washed and set	Je voudrais un shampooing – mise en plis
Set it without rollers/ on large/small rollers	Une mise en plis sans rouleaux/ avec gros/petits rouleaux
Please do not use any hairspray	N'utilisez pas de laque, s'il vous plaît
I want a colour rinse	Je voudrais un rinçage
I'd like to see a colour chart	Puis-je voir la gamme des coloris?
I want a darker/lighter shade	Je voudrais une teinte plus foncée/plus claire
I want a tint/a perm	Je voudrais un colorant/une permanente
The water is too cold	L'eau est trop froide
The dryer is too hot	Le séchoir est trop chaud
Thank you, I like it very much	Merci, c'est très bien
I want a manicure	Je voudrais un manucure

Hardware

Where is the camping equipment?	Où se trouve le matériel de camping?
Do you have a battery for this?	Avez-vous une pile pour cet appareil?
Where can I get butane gas/paraffin?	Où pourrais-je trouver du gaz butane/du pétrole?
I need a bottle opener/tin opener/corkscrew	J'ai besoin d'un décapsuleur/d'un ouvre-boîte/d'un tire-bouchon
A small/large screwdriver	Un petit/grand tournevis
I'd like some candles/matches	Je voudrais des bougies/des allumettes
I want a flashlight/pen-knife/pair of scissors	Je veux une lampe de poche/un canif/une paire de ciseaux
Do you sell string/rope?	Vous vendez de la ficelle/de la corde?
Where can I find washing-up liquid/scouring powder/soap pads?	Où puis-je trouver du liquide pour la vaisselle/de la poudre à récurer/des tampons à récurer
Do you have a dishcloth/brush?	Avez-vous un torchon/une brosse?
I need a groundsheet/bucket/frying pan	J'ai besoin d'un tapis de sol/d'un seau/d'une poêle à frire

Laundry and dry cleaning

Where is the nearest launderette/ dry cleaner?

Où se trouve la laverie/la teinturerie la plus proche?

I want to have these things washed/cleaned

Je voudrais faire laver/faire nettoyer ces affaires

Can you get this stain out?

Pouvez-vous faire disparaître cette tâche?

It is coffee/wine/grease

C'est du café/du vin/de la graisse

It only needs to be pressed

Ceci n'a besoin que d'être repassé

This is torn; can you mend it?

Ceci est déchiré; pouvez-vous le réparer?

Do you do invisible mending?

Est-ce que vous faites le stoppage?

There's a button missing

Il manque un bouton

Will you sew on another one, please?

Pouvez-vous le remplacer, s'il vous plaît?

When will it be ready?

Quand est-ce que ce sera prêt?

I need them by this evening/ tomorrow

J'en ai besoin pour ce soir/pour demain

Call back at 5 o'clock

*Revenez vers cinq heures

We can't do it before Tuesday

*Nous ne pouvons pas le faire avant mardi

It will take three days

*Cela prendra trois jours

Newspapers, writing materials and records

Do you sell English/American newspapers/magazines?	Avez-vous des journaux/des périodiques anglais/américains?
Can you get . . . for me?	Pourriez-vous faire venir . . . pour moi?
Where can I get the . . .?	Où pourrais-je trouver le . . .?
I want a map of the city/road map of . . .	Je voudrais un plan de la ville/ une carte de . . .
I want an entertainment/ amusements guide[1]	Je voudrais un guide des spectacles
Do you have any English books?	Avez-vous des livres anglais?
Have you any books by . . .?	Avez-vous des livres de . . .?
I want some coloured/black and white postcards	Je voudrais des cartes postales en couleurs/en noir et blanc
Do you sell souvenirs/toys?	Est-ce que vous vendez des souvenirs/des jouets?
Do you have any records of local music?	Avez vous des disques de musique locale?
Are there any new records by . . .?	Y a-t-il des disques nouveaux de . . .?
Can I listen to this record, please?	Puis-je écouter ce disque, s'il vous plaît?
Ballpoint	Le crayon à bille
Sellotape	Le ruban adhésif

1. In Paris, the equivalent to *What's on in London* is called *La semaine de Paris*.

Drawing pin	La punaise
Elastic band	L'élastique *m*
Envelope	L'enveloppe *f*
Glue	La colle
Ink	L'encre *f*
(Coloured) pencil	Le crayon (de couleur)
String	La ficelle
(Writing) paper	Le papier (à lettre)

Photography

I want to buy a camera	Je voudrais acheter un appareil photographique
Have you a film/cartridge for this camera?	Avez-vous des pellicules/des chargeurs pour cet appareil?
Give me a 35 mm. film with 20/36 exposures	Donnez-moi un film de trente-cinq millimètres, vingt/trente-six poses
I want a (fast) colour film/ black-and-white film	Je voudrais une pellicule couleur/ noir et blanc (rapide)
Would you fit the film in the camera for me, please?	Pouvez-vous charger l'appareil, s'il vous plaît?
How much is it?	C'est combien?
Does the price include processing?	Est-ce que le développement est compris dans le prix?

I'd like this film developed and printed	Je voudrais faire développer et tirer ce film
Please enlarge this negative	Pouvez-vous agrandir ce négatif, s'il vous plaît
When will it be ready?	Quand est-ce que ce sera prêt?
Will it be done tomorrow?	Est-ce que ce sera fait demain?
Do you have flash bulbs/cubes?	Avez-vous des ampoules-flash/ des cubes-flash?
My camera's not working, can you mend it?	Mon appareil ne marche pas, pouvez-vous le réparer?
The film is jammed	La pellicule est bloquée
There is something wrong with the shutter/light meter/film winder	L'obturateur/la cellule/l'enrouleur ne marche pas
I need a (haze) filter/lens cap	Je voudrais un filtre (de brume)/ un capuchon d'objectif

Tobacconist[1]

Do you stock English/American cigarettes?	Avez-vous des cigarettes anglaises/américaines?
What cigarettes have you?	Quelles marques de cigarettes avez-vous?
A packet of . . ., please	Un paquet de . . ., s'il vous plaît

1. Tobacconists in France also sell postage stamps.

I want some filter tip cigarettes/cigarettes without filter/mentholated cigarettes	Je voudrais des cigarettes à bout filtre/des cigarettes sans filtre/des cigarettes mentholées
A box of matches, please	Une boîte d'allumettes, s'il vous plaît
Do you have cigarette papers/pipe cleaners?	Vendez-vous du papier à cigarette/des nettoie-pipes?
I want to buy a lighter	Je voudrais acheter un briquet
Do you sell lighter fuel/flints?	Vendez-vous de l'essence pour briquet/des pierres à briquet?
I want a gas refill for this lighter	Je voudrais une recharge de gaz pour ce briquet

Repairs

This is broken; could somebody mend it?	Ceci est cassé; est-ce qu'on peut le réparer?
Could you do it while I wait?	Pouvez-vous le faire tout de suite?
When should I come back for it?	Quand dois-je revenir le/la chercher?
I want these shoes soled	Je voudrais faire ressemeler ces chaussures
I want leather soles	Je voudrais des semelles en cuir
I want these shoes heeled with rubber	Je voudrais faire mettre des talons en caoutchouc à cette paire de chaussures

I have broken the heel; can you put on a new one?	J'ai cassé le talon; pouvez-vous le remplacer?
My watch is broken	Ma montre est cassée
I have broken the glass/strap/spring	J'ai cassé le verre/le bracelet/le ressort
I have broken my glasses/the frame/the arm	J'ai cassé mes lunettes/la monture/la branche
How much would a new one cost?	Un neuf/une neuve me coûterait combien?
The stone/charm/screw has come loose	Le pierre/l'amulette/la vis est desserré(e)
The fastener/clip/chain is broken	Le fermoir/la pince/la chaine est cassé(e)
It can't be repaired	*C'est irréparable

Post Office

Where's the main post office?	Où est le bureau de poste principal?
Where's the nearest post office?	Où est le bureau de poste le plus proche?
What time does the post office open/close	À quelle heure ouvre/ferme le bureau de poste?
Where's the post box?	Où est la boîte aux lettres?
Which window do I go to for stamps/telegrams/money orders?	À quel guichet faut-il s'adresser pour les timbres/télégrammes/mandats?

Letters and telegrams[1]

How much is a postcard to England	À combien faut-il affranchir une carte postale pour l'Angleterre?
What's the airmail to the USA?	À combien faut-il affranchir une lettre avion pour les États-Unis?
How much is it to send a letter surface mail to the USA?	À combien faut-il affranchir une lettre pour les États-Unis par la voie ordinaire?
It's for France	C'est pour la France
Give me three . . . franc stamps, please	Donnez-moi trois timbres à . . . francs, s'il vous plaît
I want to send this letter express	Je voudrais envoyer cette lettre exprès
I want to register this letter	Je voudrais recommander cette lettre
Where is the poste restante section?	Où est le guichet de la poste restante?
Are there any letters for me?	Y a-t-il du courrier pour moi?
What is your name?	*Comment vous appelez-vous?
Have you any means of identification?	*Avez-vous une pièce d'identité?

1. In France stamps are on sale in tobacconists and newsagents as well as in post offices. In the Paris postal region an express letter (*un pneumatique*) can be sent by pneumatic tube from any post office.

I want to send a (reply paid) telegram	Je voudrais envoyer un télégramme (réponse payée)
How much does it cost per word?	C'est combien le mot?
Write the message here and your own name and address	*Écrivez le texte ici et mettez votre nom et votre adresse

Telephoning[1]

Where's the nearest phone box?	Où est la cabine téléphonique la plus proche?
I want to make a phone call	Je voudrais donner un coup de téléphone
May I use your phone?	Puis-je utiliser votre téléphone?
Do you have a telephone directory for ...?	Avez-vous un annuaire des téléphones pour ...?
Please give me a token	Donnez-moi un jeton, s'il vous plaît
Please get me ...	Donnez-moi le ...
I want to telephone to England	Je voudrais téléphoner en Angleterre

1. Telephone boxes are found in post offices, in public places, e.g. stations, streets, town squares. All call boxes take one franc or fifty centime coins; some also take five franc coins. Card phones are now being introduced. These operate with cards which can be bought from post offices, and tobacconists and newspaper kiosks in stations. To make an international call dial 19 and wait for a continuous dialling tone; then dial the code of the country required (44 for Great Britain), then the town code, omitting the initial 0 if there is one (so 1 for London), then the subscriber's number.

I want to place a personal (*person-to-person*) call	Je voudrais faire un appel avec préavis
Could you give me the cost (*time and charges*) afterwards?	Pourriez-vous me donner ensuite la durée et le coût de la communication?
I want to reverse the charges (*call collect*)	Je voudrais une communication en p.c.v. (*pay say vay*)
I was cut off, can you reconnect me?	J'ai été coupé, pouvez-vous me redonner la communication?
Hallo	Allô
I want extension 43	Je voudrais le poste quarante-trois
May I speak to . . .	Pourrais-je parler à . . .
Who's speaking?	*Qui est à l'appareil, s'il vous plaît?
Hold the line, please	*Ne quittez pas
Put the receiver down	*Raccrochez
He's not here	*Il n'est pas là
He's at . . .	*Il est à . . .
When will he be back?	Quand sera-t-il de retour?
Will you take a message?	Voulez-vous prendre un message?
Tell him that . . . phoned	Dites-lui que . . . a téléphoné
I'll ring again later	Je rappellerai plus tard
Please ask him to phone me	Demandez-lui de me rappeler, s'il vous plaît

What's your number	*Quel est votre numéro?
My number is . . .	Mon numéro est . . .
I can't hear you	Je vous entends très mal
The line is engaged	*La ligne est occupée
There's no reply	*Il n'y a pas de réponse/le numéro ne répond pas
You have the wrong number	*Vous vous êtes trompé de numéro
The number you dialled does not exist (recorded message)	*Il n'y a pas d'abonné au numéro que vous avez demandé

Sightseeing[1]

What ought one to see here?	Que faut-il visiter ici?
Is there a sightseeing tour/boat ride?	Y a-t-il une visite touristique/une excursion en bateau?
What's this building?	Quel est ce ce bâtiment?
Which is the oldest building in the city?	Quel est le plus vieux monument de la ville?
When was it built?	Quand a-t-il été construit?
Who built it?	Qui l'a construit?
What's the name of this church?	Comment s'appelle cette église?
What time is mass/the service at . . . church?	À quelle heure a lieu la messe/ l'office à l'église . . .?
Is this the natural history museum?	Est-ce bien le museum d'histoire naturelle?
When is the museum open?	Quelles sont les heures d'ouverture du musée?
Is it open on Sundays?	Est-il ouvert le dimanche?

1. See also BUS and COACH TRAVEL (p. 49), DIRECTIONS (p. 52).

The museum is closed on Tuesdays[1]	*Le musée est fermé le mardi
Admission free	*Entrée libre/gratuite
How much is it to go in?	Combien coûte l'entrée?
Are there reductions for children/students?	Y a-t-il des réductions pour enfants/pour étudiants?
Are the entry fees reduced on any special day?	Est-ce que le tarif d'entrée est réduit certains jours de la semaine?
Have you a ticket?	*Avez-vous un billet?
Where do I get tickets?	Où achète-t-on les billets?
Please leave your bag in the cloakroom	*Veuillez déposer votre sac au vestiaire
It's over there	*C'est là-bas
Can I take pictures?	Est-ce que je peux prendre des photos?
Cameras are prohibited	*Les appareils de photo sont interdits
Follow the guide	*Suivez le guide
Does the guide speak English?	Est-ce que le guide parle anglais?
We don't need a guide	Nous n'avons pas besoin de guide
Where is the . . . collection/exhibition?	Où se trouve la collection/l'exposition . . .?
Where are the Rembrandts?	Où sont les Rembrandt?

1. Most Paris museums open at 10 a.m. and close at 5 p.m.; elsewhere the hours are likely to be 10 to noon and 2 to 5 p.m. In and around Paris Tuesday is the usual closing day; in other cities it is Monday.

Where can I get a catalogue?	Où puis-je me procurer un catalogue?
Where can I get a plan/guide book of the city?	Où puis-je trouver un plan/un guide de la ville?
Is this the way to the zoo?	Est-ce la bonne direction pour aller au zoo?
Which bus goes to the castle?	Quel autobus va au château?
How do I get to the park?	Comment puis-je me rendre au parc?
Where do we find antiques/ souvenirs/a shopping centre/ the market?	Où pouvons-nous trouver des antiquités/des souvenirs/un centre commercial/le marché?
Can we walk there?	Pouvons-nous y aller à pied?

Entertainment

Is there an entertainment guide?	Y a-t-il un guide des spectacles?
What's on at the theatre/cinema?[1]	Qu'est-ce qu'on joue au théâtre/au cinéma?
Is there a concert?	Est-ce qu'il y a un concert?
I want two seats for tonight/for the matinée tomorrow	Je voudrais deux places pour ce soir/pour la matinée de demain
I want to book seats for Thursday	Je voudrais louer des places pour jeudi
We're sold out (for that performance)	*Tout est complet (pour cette représentation)
Are they good seats?	Est-ce que ce sont de bonnes places?
Where are these seats?	Où sont ces places?

1. Theatres always close one day each week, but are open for the matinée performance on Sundays. Seats can be reserved at the theatre every day from 11 a.m. to 5 p.m.; they are normally only on sale about a week before any given performance. Cinemas in Paris and other large French cities are open from 2 p.m. to midnight. Many have set hours for performances, the others are *cinémas permanents* – i.e. performances are continuous.

When does the curtain go up?	Le lever du rideau est à quelle heure?
What time does the performance end?	À quelle heure finit le spectacle?
Is evening dress necessary?	Est-ce que la tenue de soirée est de rigueur?
Where is the cloakroom?	Où est le vestiaire?
This is your seat	*Voici votre place¹
A programme, please	Un programme, s'il vous plaît
What's the best nightclub?	Quel est le meilleur cabaret/ nightclub?
What time is the floorshow?	À quelle heure commencent les attractions?
May I have this dance?	Voulez-vous m'accorder cette danse?
	more familiar: Vous dansez, mademoiselle?
Is there a jazz club here?	Y a-t-il un club de jazz ici?
Do you have a discotheque here?	Y a-t-il une discothèque ici?
Can you recommend a good show?	Pouvez-vous recommander un bon spectacle?

1. It is usual to tip the ouvreuse (usherette) in both theatre and cinema.

Sports and games

Where is the nearest tennis court/golf course?	Où est le court de tennis/le terrain de golf le plus proche?
What is the charge per game/hour/day?	Quel est le tarif de la partie/de l'heure/de la journée?
Where can we go swimming/fishing?	Où peut-on aller se baigner/pêcher?
Can I hire a racket/clubs/fishing tackle?	Puis-je louer une raquette/des clubs/du matériel de pêche?
Do I need a permit?	Est-ce que j'ai besoin d'un permis?
Is there a skating rink/ski slope?	Y a-t-il une patinoire/une piste de ski?
Can I hire skates/skiing equipment?	Puis-je louer des patins à glace/du matériel de ski?
Are there ski lifts?	Y a-t-il des remonte-pentes?
Can I take lessons here?	Puis-je prendre des leçons ici?
Clay-pigeon shooting	Le ball-trap

Where is the stadium?	Où est le stade?
Are there any seats left in the grandstand?	Reste-t-il des places aux tribunes?
How much are the cheapest seats?	Combien valent les places les moins chères?
Are the seats in the sun/shade?	Y a-t-il des places au soleil/à l'ombre?
We want to go to a football match/the tennis tournament/ a bullfight	Nous voulons aller voir un match de football/le tournoi de tennis/une course de taureaux
Who's playing?	Qui est-ce qui joue?
When does it start?	À quelle heure est-ce que cela commence?
What is the score?	Quel est le score (*rugby and soccer*)/Où en est la partie? (*tennis*)
Who's winning?	Qui gagne?
Where's the race course?	Où est le champ de courses/ l'hippodrome?
When's the next meeting?	Quand a lieu la prochaine réunion?
Which is the favourite?	Quel est le favori?
Who's the jockey?	Qui est le jockey?
10 francs to win on . . .[1]	Dix francs gagnant sur . . .

1. The equivalent of the tote in France is the P.M.U. (Pari Mutuel Urbain). Bets can be placed at the offices at a race course or at any café or tobacconist with the sign P.M.U.

10 francs each way on . . .

Dix francs gagnant, dix francs placé sur . . .

What are the odds?

Quelle est la cote?

Do you play cards?

Jouez-vous aux cartes?

Would you like a game of chess?

Cela vous dit de faire une partie d'échecs?

I'd like to play a game of checkers (draughts)

J'aimerais faire une partie de dames

On the beach

Which is the best beach?	Quelle est la meilleure plage?
Is there a quiet beach near here?	Y a-t-il une plage tranquille près d'ici?
Is it far to walk?	Est-ce loin à pied?
Is there a bus to the beach?	Y a-t-il un autobus qui va à la plage?
Is the beach sand or shingle?	Est-ce une plage de sable ou de galets?
Is the bathing dangerous from this beach/bay?	Est-ce qu'il est dangereux de se baigner sur cette plage/dans cette baie?
Is it safe for small children?	La plage est-elle sûre pour les jeunes enfants?
Bathing prohibited	*Baignade interdite
It's dangerous	*C'est dangereux
Is the tide rising/falling?	Est-ce que la marée monte/descend?

Does the sea get very rough?	La mer peut–elle être très mauvaise ici?
There's a strong current here	*Le courant est violent ici
You will be out of your depth	*Vous n'aurez pas pied
Are you a strong swimmer?	*Êtes-vous bon nageur?
Is it deep?	Est-ce que c'est profond?
How's the water? Cold?	Est-ce que l'eau est froide?
It's warm	Elle est chaude/bonne
Can one swim in the lake/river?[1]	Peut-on se baigner dans le lac/le fleuve/la rivière?
Is there an indoor/outdoor swimming pool?	Y a-t-il une piscine couverte/ en plein air?
Is it salt or fresh water?	Est-ce de l'eau salée ou de l'eau douce?
Are there showers?	Y a-t-il des douches?
I want to hire a cabin for the day/morning/two hours	Je voudrais louer une cabine pour la journée/pour la matinée/pour deux heures
I want to hire a deckchair/ sunshade	Je voudrais louer une chaise longue/un parasol
Can we water ski here?	Peut-on faire du ski nautique ici?
Can we hire the equipment?	Peut-on louer l'équipement?
Where's the harbour?	Où est le port?

1. There are two words for 'river' in French. *Fleuve* is used for rivers that flow into the sea and *rivière* for rivers that flow into *fleuves*.

Can we go out in a fishing boat?	Peut-on aller faire une promenade en bateau de pêche?
Is there any underwater fishing?	Est-ce qu'on fait de la pêche sous-marine ici?
Can I hire skin-diving equipment/a snorkel/flippers?	Puis-je louer l'équipement de plongée sous-marine/ un tuba/ des palmes?
Can I hire a rowing boat/motor boat?	Peut-on louer un bateau à rames/un canot à moteur?
What does it cost by the hour?	Combien coûte l'heure de location?

Camping and walking [1]

How long is the walk to the Youth Hostel?	Combien de temps faut-il pour aller à l'Auberge de Jeunesse à pied?
How far is the next village?	À quelle distance se trouve le prochain village?
Is there a footpath to . . .?	Y a-t-il un sentier qui mène à . . .?
Is it possible to go there across country?	Est-il possible d'y aller à travers champs?
Is there a short cut?	Y a-t-il un raccourci?
It's an hour's walk to . . .	*Il faut une heure de marche pour aller à . . .
Is there a camping site near here?	Y a-t-il un terrain de camping près d'ici?
Is this an authorized camp site?	Est-ce un terrain de camping officiel?

1. See also DIRECTIONS (p. 52).

Is drinking water/are lavatories/ showers provided?	Y a-t-il de l'eau potable/des toilettes/des douches?
May we camp here?	Pouvons-nous camper ici?
Can we hire a tent?	Peut-on louer une tente?
Can we park our caravan here?	Peut-on garer la caravane ici?
What does it cost per person/day/ week?	Quelle est la redevance perçue par personne/pour un jour/pour une semaine?
What is the charge for a tent/ caravan?	Quelle est la redevance perçue pour une tente/une caravane?
Is this drinking water?	Est-ce que cette eau est potable?
Where are the shops?	Où sont les magasins?
Where can I buy paraffin/butane gas?	Où puis-je acheter du pétrole/du gaz butane?
May we light a fire?	Pouvons-nous faire du feu?
Where do I get rid of rubbish?	Où puis-je vider les ordures?

At the doctor's

Ailments

Is there a doctor's surgery near here? — Y a-t-il un cabinet de consultation près d'ici?

I must see a doctor, can you recommend one? — Il faut que je consulte un médecin; pouvez-vous m'en recommander un?

Please call a doctor — Faites venir un médecin, s'il vous plaît

I am ill — Je suis malade

I have a fever — J'ai la fièvre

I've a pain in my right arm — J'ai une douleur au bras droit

My wrist hurts — Mon poignet me fait mal

I think I've sprained/broken my ankle — Je crois que je me suis foulé/cassé la cheville

I fell down and hurt my back — Je suis tombé et je me suis fait mal au dos

My foot is swollen	Mon pied est enflé
I've burned/cut/hurt myself	Je me suis brûlé/coupé/fait mal
My stomach[1] is upset	J'ai mal au ventre
My appetite's gone	Je n'ai plus d'appétit
I think I've got food poisoning	Je crois souffrir d'une intoxication alimentaire
I can't eat/sleep	Je ne peux pas manger/dormir
My nose keeps bleeding	Je saigne constamment du nez
I have earache	J'ai mal à l'oreille (*one ear*)/aux oreilles (*both*)
I have difficulty in breathing	J'ai du mal à respirer
I feel dizzy/sick/shivery	J'ai des vertiges/nausées/frissons
I keep vomiting	Je vomis souvent
I think I've caught 'flu	Je crois que j'ai attrapé la grippe
I've got a cold	Je suis enrhumé
I've had it since yesterday/for a few hours	J'ai cela depuis hier/depuis quelques heures

abscess	l'abcès *m*	lab-se
ache	le mal/la douleur	mal/doo-lœr
allergy	l'allergie *f*	lal-air-zhee
appendicitis	l'appendicite *f*	la-pahⁿ-dee-seet
asthma	l'asthme *m*	as-me

1. 'Stomach' in English is used loosely to apply to the abdomen. The French word *estomac* has a stricter anatomical meaning.

blister	l'ampoule *f*	lahⁿ-pool

blister	l'ampoule *f*	lah^n-pool
boil	le furoncle	fu^e-roh^{n}kl
bruise	le bleu/la contusion	ble^r/koh^n-tu^e-zyoh^n
burn	la brûlure	bru^e-lu^{e}r
chill	le refroidissement	re-frwa-dees-mah^n
cold	le rhume	ru^{e}m
constipation	la constipation	koh^n-stee-pa-syoh^n
cough	la toux	too
cramp	la crampe	krah^{n}p
diabetic	diabétique	dya-bay-teek
diarrhoea	la diarrhée	dya-ray
earache	le mal à l'oreille	mal a lor-ay
fever	la fièvre	fyevr
food poisoning	l'intoxication alimentaire	la^n-toks-ee-ka-syoh^n al-ee-mah^n-tair
fracture	la fracture	frak-tu^{e}r
hay-fever	le rhume des foins	ru^{e}m day fwa^n
headache	le mal de tête	mal de^r tet
ill/sick	malade	ma-lad
illness	la maladie	ma-lad-ee
indigestion	l'indigestion *f*	la^n-dee-zhest-yoh^n
infection	l'infection *f*	la^n-fek-syoh^n
influenza	la grippe	greep
insomnia	l'insomnie *f*	la^n-som-nee

itch	la démangeaison	day-mahn-zhay-zohn
nausea	la nausée	noh-zay
pain	la douleur	doo-lœr
rheumatism	le rhumatisme	rue-ma-teesm
sore throat	le mal de gorge/ l'angine	mal der gorzh/ lahn-zheen
sprain	la foulure	foo-luer
stomach ache	le mal au ventre	mal oh vahntr
sunburn	le coup de soleil	koo der sol-ay
sunstroke	l'insolation f	lan-so-la-syohn
tonsillitis	l'angine f	ahn-zheen
toothache	le mal aux dents	mal oh dahn
ulcer	l'ulcère m	uel-sair
wound	la blessure	bles-uer

Treatment

You're hurting me	Vous me faites mal
Must I stay in bed?	Dois-je garder le lit?
Will you call again?	Est-ce que vous repasserez me voir?
How much do I owe you?	Combien vous dois-je?
When can I travel again?	Quand pourrai-je repartir?
I feel better now	Je me sens mieux maintenant

Do you have a temperature?	*Faites-vous de la température?
Where does it hurt?	*Où avez-vous mal?
Have you a pain here?	*Avez-vous mal là?
How long have you had the pain?	*Depuis quand avez-vous cette douleur?
Open your mouth	*Ouvrez la bouche
Put out your tongue	*Montrez-moi votre langue
Breathe in	*Respirez/inspirez
Breathe out	*Soufflez/expirez
Does that hurt?	*Est-ce que cela vous fait mal?
A lot?/A little?	*Très mal?/Un peu?
Please lie down	*Allongez-vous, s'il vous plaît
I will need a specimen	*J'ai besoin d'un spécimen (de vos urines)
You must have a blood/urine test	*Vous devez faire faire des analyses de sang/d'urine
What medicine have you been taking?	*Quels médicaments/remèdes prenez-vous?
I take this medicine – could you give me another prescription?	Je prends ce médicament – pourriez-vous m'établir une nouvelle ordonnance?
I'll give you some pills/medicine	*Je vais vous donner des pilules/des médicaments
I will give you an antibiotic/sedative	*Je vais vous donner un antibiotique/un calmant
Take this prescription to the chemist's	*Allez chez le pharmacien avec cette ordonnance

Take this three times a day	*Prenez ceci trois fois par jour
I'll give you an injection	*Je vais vous faire une piqûre
Roll up your sleeve	*Retroussez votre manche
I'll put you on a diet	*Je vais vous mettre au régime
Come and see me again in two days' time	*Revenez me voir dans deux jours
You leg must be X-rayed	*Il faut faire radiographier votre jambe
You must go to hospital	*Il faut que vous alliez à l'hôpital
You must stay in bed	*Vous devez rester au lit
You should not travel until …	*Vous ne devriez pas voyager avant …
Nothing to worry about	*Ce n'est pas grave/Ce n'est rien

ambulance	l'ambulance *f*	lah^n-bue-lah^{n}s
anaesthetic	l'anesthésique *m*	lanes-tay-zeek
aspirin	l'aspirine *f*	las-peer-een
bandage	le pansement/la bande	pah^n-smah^n/bah^{n}d
chiropodist	le pédicure	pay-dee-ku^{e}r
hospital	l'hôpital *m*	lop-ee-tal
injection	la piqûre	pee-ku^{e}r
laxative	le laxatif	lak-sa-teef
nurse	l'infirmière *f*	lah^n-fairm-yair
operation	l'opération *f*	lop-ay-ra-syoh^n
optician	l'opticien *m*	lop-tee-sya^n

osteopath	l'ostéopathe *m*	los-tay-o-pat
pill	la pilule	pee-lu^{e}l
(adhesive) plaster	le sparadrap/le tricostéril	spa-ra-dra/tree-ko-stair-eel
prescription	l'ordonnance *f*	lor-don-ah^{n}s
X-ray	la radio (-graphie)	ra-dyo-graf-ee

Parts of the body

ankle	la cheville	she^r-vee-y
arm	le bras	bra
back	le dos	doh
bladder	la vessie	vay-see
blood	le sang	sah^n
body	le corps	kor
bone	l'os *m*	los
bowels	les intestins *m*	a^n-test-a^n
brain	le cerveau	sair-voh
breast	le sein	sa^n
cheek	la joue	zhoo
chest	la poitrine	pwa-treen
chin	le menton	mah^n-toh^n
collar-bone	la clavicule	kla-vee-ku^{e}l

ear	l'oreille *f*	lor-ay
elbow	le coude	kood
eye	l'œil *m* (*pl* les yeux)	lœ-y (layz-yœ)
eyelid	la paupière	poh-pyair
face	la figure	fee-gu^{e}r
finger	le doigt	dwa
foot	le pied	pyay
forehead	le front	froh^n
gall bladder	la vésicule (biliaire)	vay-zee-ku^{e}l (bee-lyair)
gum	la gencive	zhah^n-seev
hand	la main	ma^n
head	la tête	tet
heart	le cœur	kœr
heel	le talon	tal-oh^n
hip	la hanche	ah^{n}sh
jaw	la mâchoire	mash-war
joint	la jointure	zhwa^n-tu^{e}r
kidney	le rein	ra^n
knee	le genou	zhe^r-noo
knee-cap	la rotule	roh-tu^{e}l
leg	la jambe	zhah^{n}b
lip	la lèvre	levr
liver	le foie	fwa
lung	le poumon	poo-moh^n

mouth	la bouche	boosh
muscle	le muscle	mu^{e}skl
nail	l'ongle *m*	loh^n-gl
neck	le cou	koo
nerve	le nerf	nair
nose	le nez	nay
rib	la côte	koht
shoulder	l'épaule *f*	lay-pohl
skin	la peau	poh
stomach	l'estomac *m*	les-to-mak
temple	la tempe	tah^{n}p
thigh	la cuisse	kwees
throat	la gorge	gorzh
thumb	le pouce	poos
toe	l'orteil *m*	lor-tay
tongue	la langue	lah^{n}g
tonsils	les amygdales *f*	lay-zam-ee-dal
tooth	la dent	dah^n
vein	la veine	ven
wrist	le poignet	pwan-yay

At the dentist's

I must see a dentist	Je dois voir un dentiste
Can I make an appointment with the dentist?	Puis-je prendre rendez-vous avec le dentiste?
As soon as possible	Le plus tôt possible
I have toothache	J'ai mal aux dents
This tooth hurts	Cette dent me fait mal
I've lost a filling	J'ai perdu un plombage
Can you fill it?	Pouvez-vous la plomber?
Can you do it now?	Pouvez-vous le faire maintenant?
I do not want the tooth taken out	Je ne veux pas que la dent soit arrachée
Please give me an injection first	Insensibilisez-moi la dent d'abord, s'il vous plaît
My gums are swollen	Mes gencives sont enflées
My gums keep bleeding	Mes gencives saignent souvent

I have broken/chipped my dentures	J'ai cassé/ébréché mon dentier
Can you fix it (temporarily)?	Pouvez-vous le réparer (provisoirement)?
You're hurting me	Vous me faites mal
How much do I owe you?	Combien vous dois-je?
When should I come again?	Quand dois-je revenir?
Please rinse your mouth	*Rincez-vous la bouche, s'il vous plaît
I will X-ray your teeth	*Je vais faire une radio de vos dents
You have an abscess	*Vous avez un abcès
The nerve is exposed	*Le nerf est à vif
This tooth can't be saved	*Cette dent est perdue

Problems and accidents

Where's the police station?[1]	Où est le commissariat de police/ la gendarmerie?
Call the police	Appelez la police
Where is the British consulate?	Où est le consulat britannique?
Please let the consulate know	Veuillez informer le consulat, s'il vous plaît
My bag has been stolen	On m'a volé mon sac
I found this in the street	J'ai trouvé ceci dans la rue
I have lost my luggage/ passport/traveller's cheques	J'ai perdu mes bagages/mon passeport/mes chèques de voyage
I have missed my train	J'ai manqué le train
My luggage is on board	Mes bagages sont à bord

1. In towns and cities police duties are performed by *agents* (*de police*), addressed as *Monsieur l'agent*. The police station is called *commissariat de police*. In very small towns and in the country police duties are performed by *gendarmes* and the police station is called the *gendarmerie*. There is a special police branch whose main duty is to patrol the roads and enforce traffic regulations. This is known as *la police de la route* and the policemen are familiarly known as *motards*.

Call a doctor	Appelez un médecin
Call an ambulance	Appelez une ambulance
There has been an accident[1]	Il y a eu un accident
He's badly hurt	Il est gravement blessé
He has fainted	Il s'est évanoui
He's losing blood	Il perd du sang
Please get some water/a blanket/some bandages	Allez chercher un peu d'eau/une couverture/des pansements, s'il vous plaît
I've broken my glasses	J'ai cassé mes lunettes
I can't see	Je ne peux pas voir
A child has fallen in the water	Un enfant est tombé à l'eau
A woman is drowning	Il y a une femme qui se noie
May I see your insurance certificate?	*Je voudrais voir votre certificat/attestation d'assurance
Apply to the insurance company	Adressez-vous à la compagnie d'assurances
Can you help me?	Pouvez-vous m'aider?
What is the name and address of the owner?	Quels sont le nom et l'adresse du propriétaire?
Are you willing to act as a witness?	Voulez-vous bien servir de témoin?

1. If you are involved in an accident in a town get the *agent de police* to make a report (*dresser un constat*). In the country if there has been injury to people, advise the *gendarmerie*. In other cases engage a *huissier* (sheriff's officer) from the nearest town to make a report. Try to get the names and addresses of witnesses.

Can I have your name and address, please?

Pourrais-je avoir votre nom et votre adresse, s'il vous plaît?

I want a copy of the police report

Je voudrais une copie du constat

There's a bus strike

*Il y a une grève des autobus

Time and dates

TIME	L'HEURE
What time is it?	Quelle heure est-il?
It's one o'clock	Il est une heure
two o'clock	deux heures
five past eight	huit heures cinq
quarter past five	cinq heures et quart
twenty-five past eight	huit heures vingt-cinq
half past four	quatre heures et demie
twenty-five to seven	sept heures moins vingt-cinq
twenty to three	trois heures moins vingt
quarter to ten	dix heures moins le quart
Second	La seconde
Minute	La minute
Hour	L'heure *f*
It's early/late	Il est tôt/tard
My watch is slow/fast/has stopped	Ma montre retarde/avance/s'est arrêtée
Sorry I'm late	(Je suis) désolé d'être en retard

DATE   LA DATE

What's the date?	Quelle est la date?
It's December 9th	Nous sommes le neuf décembre
We're leaving on January 5th[1]	Nous partons le cinq janvier
We got here on July 27th	Nous sommes arrivés le vingt-sept juillet

DAY   LE JOUR/LA JOURNÉE   zhoor/zhoor-nay

Morning	le matin/la matinée	ma-ta^n/ma-tee-nay
this morning	ce matin	se^r ma-ta^n
in the morning	dans la matinée	dah^n la ma-tee-nay
Midday, noon	midi	mee-dee
Afternoon	l'après-midi *m* or *f*	lapre-meedee
yesterday afternoon	hier après-midi	yair apre-meedee
Evening	le soir/la soirée	swar/swar-ay
tomorrow evening	demain soir	de^r-ma^n swar
Midnight	minuit	meen-wee
Night	la nuit	nwee
at night	de nuit	de^r nwee
by day	de jour	de^r zhoor
Sunrise	le lever du soleil	le^r-vay du^e so-lay
at sunrise	au lever du soleil	oh le^r-vay du^e so-lay

1. In French, cardinal numbers are used for dates except for the first, for which *premier* is used.

Dawn	l'aube/l'aurore *f*	lohb/lor-or
at dawn	au point du jour	oh pwa^n du^e zhoor
Sunset	le coucher du soleil	koo-shay du^e so-lay
Dusk	le crépuscule	kray-pu^{e}s-ku^{e}l
Today	aujourd'hui	oh-zhoor-dwee
Yesterday	hier	yair
day before yesterday	avant-hier	avah^n tyair
Tomorrow	demain	de^r-ma^n
day after tomorrow	après-demain	a-pre de^r-ma^n
In ten days' time	dans dix jours	dah^n dee zhoor
WEEK	LA SEMAINE	se^r-men
Monday	lundi	le^n-dee
Tuesday	mardi	mar-dee
Wednesday	mercredi	mair-kre^r-dee
Thursday	jeudi	zhe^r-dee
Friday	vendredi	vah^n-dre^r-dee
Saturday	samedi	sam-dee
Sunday	dimanche	dee-mah^{n}sh
on Tuesday	mardi	mar-dee
on Sundays	le dimanche	le^r dee-mah^{n}sh
Fortnight	une quinzaine	ka^n-zen

MONTH	LE MOIS	mwa
January	janvier	zhahn-vyay
February	février	fay-vryay
March	mars	mars
April	avril	a-vreel
May	mai	me
June	juin	zhwahn
July	juillet	zhwee-ye
August	août	oo
September	septembre	sep-tahnbr
October	octobre	okt-obr
November	novembre	nov-ahnbr
December	décembre	day-sahnbr
in January	en janvier	ahn zhahn-vyay

SEASON	LE SAISON	se-zohn
Spring	le printemps	pran-tahn
Summer	l'été *m*	lay-tay
Autumn	l'automne *m or f*	loh-tahn
Winter	l'hiver *m*	lee-vair
in spring	au printemps	oh pran-tahn
in summer/ autumn/winter	en été/automne/ hiver	ahn ay-tay/oh-tahn/ ee-vair
during the summer	pendant l'été	pahn-dahn lay-tay

YEAR	L'AN/L'ANNÉE	lahⁿ/la-nay

This year	cette année	set a-nay
Last year	l'année dernière	la-nay dair-nyair
Next year	l'année prochaine	la-nay pro-shen

Public holidays

1 January	Le jour de l'an	New Year's Day
	Le vendredi saint	Good Friday (Switzerland only)
	Le lundi de Pâques	Easter Monday
1 May	La fête du Travail	Labour Day
	L'Ascension	Ascension Day (sixth Thursday after Easter)
	Le lundi de Pentecôte	Whit Monday
14 July	La fête nationale	Bastille Day (France only)
21 July	"	National holiday (Belgium only)
15 August	L'Assomption	The Ascension of the Virgin
1 November	La Toussaint	All Saints
11 November	Anniversaire de l'Armistice	Armistice Day
15 November	"	" (Belgium only)

| 25 December | Le jour de Noël | Christmas Day |
| 26 December | Le lendemain de Noël | Boxing Day |

Switzerland has neither Labour nor Armistice Day, nor (apart from the Italian-speaking south) the Catholic days Ascension and All Saints.

Numbers

CARDINAL

0	zéro	zay-roh
1	un	e^n
2	deux	de^r
3	trois	trwa
4	quatre	katr
5	cinq	sa^{n}k
6	six	sees
7	sept	set
8	huit	weet
9	neuf	nœf
10	dix	dees
11	onze	oh^{n}z
12	douze	dooz
13	treize	trez
14	quatorze	katorz

15	quinze	ka[n]z
16	seize	sez
17	dix-sept	dees-set
18	dix-huit	dees-weet
19	dix-neuf	dees-nœf
20	vingt	va[n]
21	vingt et un	va[n]-tay-e[n]
22	vingt-deux	va[n]-de[r]
30	trente	trah[n]t
31	trente et un	trah[n]t-ay-e[n]
32	trente-deux	trah[n]t-de[r]
40	quarante	karah[n]t
41	quarante et un	karah[n]t-ay-e[n]
42	quarante deux	karah[n]t-de[r]
50	cinquante	sa[n]kah[n]t
51	cinquante et un	sa[n] kah[n]t-ay-e[n]
52	cinquante-deux	sa[n]kah[n]t-de[r]
60	soixante	swasah[n]t
61	soixante et un	swasah[n]t-ay-e[n]
62	soixante-deux	swasah[n]t-de[r]
70	soixante-dix	swasah[n]t-dees
71	soixante et onze	swasah[n]t-ay-oh[n]z
72	soixante-douze	swasah[n]t-dooz
80	quatre-vingts	katr-va[n]

81	quatre-vingt-un	katr-van-en
82	quatre-vingt-deux	katr-van-der
90	quatre-vingt-dix	katr-van-dees
91	quatre-vingt-onze	katr-van-ohnz
92	quatre-vingt-douze	katr-van-dooz
100	cent	sahn
101	cent un	sahn en
200	deux cents	der sahn
1000	mille	meel
2000	deux mille	der meel
1,000,000	un million	mee-lyon

ORDINAL

1st	premier	prerm-yay
2nd	deuxième/second	der-zyem/segohn
3rd	troisième	trwa-zyem
4th	quatrième	kat-ryem
5th	cinquième	san-kyem
6th	sixième	se-zyem
7th	septième	se-tyem
8th	huitième	wee-tyem
9th	neuvième	ner-vyem
10th	dixième	dee-zyem
11th	onzième	ohn-zyem
12th	douzième	doo-zyem

13th	treizième	tre-zyem
14th	quatorzième	kator-zyem
15th	quinzième	ka^n-zyem
16th	seizième	se-zyem
17th	dix-septième	dees-se-tyem
18th	dix-huitième	dees-wee-tyem
19th	dix-neuvième	dees-ne^r-vyem
20th	vingtième	va^n-tyem
21st	vingt et unième	va^n-tay-u^e-nee-em
30th	trentième	trah^n-tyem
40th	quarantième	karan-tyem
50th	cinquantième	sa^{n}kah^n-tyem
60th	soixantième	swasah^n-tyem
70th	soixante-dixième	swasah^n-dee-zyem
80th	quatre-vingtième	katr-va^n-tyem
90th	quatre-vingt-dixième	katr-va^n-dee-zyem
100th	centième	sah^n-tyem
half	demi	de-mee
quarter	quart	kar
three quarters	trois quarts	trwa kar
a third	un tiers	tyair
two thirds	deux tiers	de^r tyair

In Belgium and Switzerland *septante, octante, nonante* = 70, 80, 90 with the intervening numbers corresponding.

Weights and measures

DISTANCE:

kilometres – miles

km.	*miles or km.*	miles	km.	*miles or km.*	miles
1·6	*1*	0·6	14·5	*9*	5·6
3·2	*2*	1·2	16·1	*10*	6·2
4·8	*3*	1·9	32·2	*20*	12·4
6·4	*4*	2·5	40·2	*25*	15·3
8	*5*	3·1	80·5	*50*	31·1
9·7	*6*	3·7	160·9	*100*	62·1
11·3	*7*	4·4	804·7	*500*	310·7
12·9	*8*	5·0			

A rough way to convert from miles to km.: divide by 5 and multiply by 8; from km. to miles: divide by 8 and multiply by 5.

LENGTH AND HEIGHT:

centimetres – inches

cm.	inch or cm.	inch	cm.	inch or cm.	inch
2·5	1	0·4	17·8	7	2·8
5·1	2	0·8	20	8	3·2
7·6	3	1·2	22·9	9	3·5
10·2	4	1·6	25·4	10	3·9
12·7	5	2·0	50·8	20	9·9
15·2	6	2·4	127	50	19·7

A rough way to convert from inches to cm.: divide by 2 and multiply by 5; from cm. to inches: divide by 5 and multiply by 2.

metres – feet

m.	ft or m.	ft	m.	ft or m.	ft
0.3	1	3·3	2·4	8	26·3
0·6	2	6·6	2·7	9	29·5
0·9	3	9·8	3	10	32·8
1·2	4	13·1	6·1	20	65·6
1·5	5	16·4	15·2	50	164
1·8	6	19·7	30·5	100	328·1
2·1	7	23			

A rough way to convert from ft to m.: divide by 10 and multiply by 3; from m. to ft: divide by 3 and multiply by 10.

metres – yards

m.	*yds or m.*	yds		m.	*yds or m.*	yds
0·9	*1*	1·1		7·3	*8*	8·8
1·8	*2*	2·2		8·2	*9*	9·8
2·7	*3*	3·3		9·1	*10*	10·9
3·7	*4*	4·4		18·3	*20*	21·9
4·6	*5*	5·5		45·7	*50*	54·7
5·5	*6*	6·6		91·4	*100*	109·4
6·4	*7*	7·7		457·2	*500*	546·8

A rough way to convert from yds to m.: subtract 10 per cent from the number of yds; from m. to yds: add 10 per cent to the number of metres.

LIQUID MEASURES:

litres – gallons

litres	*galls or litres*	galls		litres	*galls or litres*	galls
4·6	*1*	0·2		36·4	*8*	1·8
9·1	*2*	0·4		40·9	*9*	2·0
13·6	*3*	0·7		45·5	*10*	2·2
18·2	*4*	0·9		90·9	*20*	4·4
22·7	*5*	1·1		136·4	*30*	6·6
27·3	*6*	1·3		181·8	*40*	8·8
31·8	*7*	1·5		227·3	*50*	11

1 pint — 0·6 litre   1 litre — 1·8 pint

A rough way to convert from galls to litres: divide by 2 and multiply by 9; from litres to galls: divide by 9 and multiply by 2.

WEIGHT:

kilogrammes – pounds

kg.	*lb. or kg.*	lb.	kg.	*lb. or kg.*	lb.
0·5	*1*	2·2	3·2	*7*	15·4
0·9	*2*	4·4	3·6	*8*	17·6
1·4	*3*	6·6	4·1	*9*	19·8
1·8	*4*	8·8	4·5	*10*	22·1
2·3	*5*	11·0	9·1	*20*	44·1
2·7	*6*	13·2	22·7	*50*	110·2

To convert from lb. to kg.: divide by 11 and multiply by 5; from kg. to lb.: divide by 5 and multiply by 11.

grammes – ounces

grammes	oz.	oz.	grammes
100	3·5	2	57·1
250	8·8	4	114·3
500	17·6	8	228·6
1000 (1 kg.)	35	16 (1 lb.)	457·2

TEMPERATURE:

centigrade – fahrenheit

centigrade °C	fahrenheit °F	centigrade °C	fahrenheit °F
0	32	20	68
5	41	30	86
10	50	40	104

To convert °F to °C: deduct 32, divide by 9, multiply by 5; to convert °C to °F: divide by 5, multiply by 9 and add 32.

Vocabulary

Various groups of specialized words are given elsewhere in this book and these words are not usually repeated in the vocabulary:

A

a, an	un/une	e^n/u^{e}n
able (to be)	pouvoir	poo-vwar
about	autour (de)	oh-toor (de^r)
above	au-dessus (de)	oh de^r-su^e (de^r)
abroad	à l'étranger	alay-tra^n-zhay
accept (to)	accepter	ak-sep-tay
accident	l'accident *m*	lak-see-dah^n
ache (to)	avoir mal (à)	avwar mal (a)
acquaintance	la connaissance	ko-ne-sah^{n}s
across	à travers	a travair
act (to)	jouer	zhoo-ay
add (to)	ajouter	azhoo-tay
address	l'adresse *f*	la-dres
admire (to)	admirer	ad-mee-ray
admission	l'accès *m*/l'entrée *f*	lak-se/lah^n-tray
advice	l'avis *m*/le(s) conseil(s)	la-vee/koh^n-say
aeroplane	l'avion *m*	lav-yoh^n
afford (to)	avoir les moyens (de)	avwar lay mwa-yah^n (de^r)
afraid	pris de peur	pree de^r pœr
after	après	a-pre
again	encore	ah^n-kor

against	contre	kohⁿtr
age	l'âge *m*	lazh
... ago	il y a ...	eel-ya
agree (to)	consentir	kohⁿ-sahⁿ-teer
ahead	en avant	on-avahⁿ
air	l'air *m*	lair
airbed	le matelas pneumatique	mate^r-lah pne^r-mat-eek
air-conditioning	la climatisation	klee-mat-eez-asyohⁿ
alike	semblable	sahⁿ-blabl
all	tout/tous	too/too
all right	bien	bee-aⁿ
allow (to)	permettre	pair-mettr
almost	presque	preske^r
alone	seul	sœl
along	le long de	le^r lohⁿ de^r
already	déjà	day-zha
also	aussi	ohsee
alter (to)	changer	shahⁿ-zhay
alternative	l'alternative *f*	lal-tair-na-teev
although	quoique	kwa-ke^r
always	toujours	too-zhoor
ambulance	l'ambulance *f*	lahⁿ-bue-lahⁿs
America	l'Amérique *f*	lamay-reek

American	américain/américaine	amay-reek-ah^n(-en)
among	parmi	par-mee
amuse (to)	amuser	amu^e-zay
amusing	amusant	amu^e-zah^n
ancient	ancien	ah^n-syah^n
and	et	ay
angry	fâché	fash-ay
animal	l'animal *m*	la-nee-mal
anniversary	l'anniversaire *m*	la-nee-vair-sair
annoyed	contrarié	koh^n-trar-yay
another	un autre/une autre	e^n ohtr/u^{e}n ohtr
answer	la réponse	ray-poh^{n}s
answer (to)	répondre	ray-poh^{n}dr
antiques	les antiquités *f*	ah^n-tee-kee-tay
any	aucun	oh-ke^n
anyone	quelqu'un	kel-ke^n
anything	quelque chose	kel-ke^r-shohz
anyway	de toute façon	de^r toot fa-soh^n
anywhere	quelque part	kel-ke^r-par
apartment	l'appartement *m*	lapar-te^r-mah^n
apologize (to)	s'excuser	sek-sku^e-zay
appetite	l'appétit *m*	la-pay-tee
appointment	le rendez-vous	rah^n-day-voo
architect	l'architecte *m*	lar-shee-tekt

architecture	l'architecture f	lar-shee-tekt-u^{e}r
area	la région/la zone	ray-zhyoh^n/zohn
arm	le bras	bra
armchair	le fauteuil	foh-tœ-y
army	l'armée f	lar-may
around	autour (de)	oh-toor (de^r)
arrange (to)	arranger	arah^n-zhay
arrival	l'arrivée f	laree-vay
arrive (to)	arriver	aree-vay
art	l'art m	lar
art gallery	la galerie d'art	gal-ay-ree dar
artist	l'artiste m, f	lar-teest
as	comme	kom
as much as	autant que	ohtah^n ke^r
as soon as	aussitôt que	ohsee-toh ke^r
as well/also	aussi	ohsee
ashtray	le cendrier	sah^n-dree-ay
ask (to)	demander	de^r-mah^n-day
asleep	endormi	ah^n-dor-mee
at	à	a
at last	enfin	ah^n-fa^n
at once	immédiatement	ee-may-dee-atmah^n
atmosphere	l'atmosphère f	lat-mos-fair
attention	l'attention f	la-tah^n-syoh^n

attractive	beau/belle	boh/bel
auction	la vente aux enchères	vah^n t oh-zah^n-shair
audience	le public	pu^e-bleek
aunt	la tante	tah^n t
Australia	l'Australie *f*	loh-stra-lee
Australian	australien/ australienne	oh-stra-lya^n (-lyen)
author	l'auteur *m*	loh-tœr
available	disponible	dees-poh-neebl
average	moyen	mwa-yen
awake	(r)éveillé	(r)ay-vay-yay
away	absent	ab-sah^n
awful	affreux	a-frœ

B

baby	le bébé	bay-bay
bachelor	le célibataire	say-leeba-tair
back	en arrière	an-ar-yair
bad	mauvais	moh-ve
bag	le sac	sak
baggage	les bagages *m*	ba-gazh
bait	l'appât *m*	la-pa
balcony	le balcon	bal-koh^n

ball *sport*	la balle	bal
ballet	le ballet	ba-lay
band	l'orchestre *m*	lor-kestr
bank	la banque	bah^{n}k
bare	nu	nu^e
basket	le panier	pan-yay
bath	la baignoire	ben-ywar
bathe (to)	se baigner	ser ben-yay
bathing cap	le bonnet (de bain)	bo-nay (der ba^n)
bathing costume/ trunks	le maillot (de bain)	ma-yoh (der ba^n)
bathroom	la salle de bains	sal der ba^n
battery	la pile/la batterie	peel/ba-tair-ee
bay	la baie	be
be (to)	être	etr
beach	la plage	plazh
beard	la barbe	barb
beautiful	beau/belle	boh/bel
because	parce que	par-sker
become (to)	devenir	der-ver-neer
bed	le lit	lee
bedroom	la chambre à coucher	shah^n-br a koo-shay
before *in time*	avant	avah^n
before *in space*	devant	dervah^n

begin (to)	commencer	kom-ah^n-say
beginning	le commencement	kom-ah^n-smah^n
behind	derrière	der-yer
Belgian	belge	belzh
Belgium	la Belgique	bel-zheek
believe (to)	croire	krwar
bell	la sonnette	so-nett
belong (to)	appartenir	apar-te^r-neer
below	au-dessous (de)	oh-de^r-soo (de^r)
belt	la ceinture	sa^n-tu^{e}r
bench	le banc	bah^n
bend	le tournant/le virage	toor-nah^n/vee-razh
beneath	sous/au dessous de	soo/oh de^r-soo de^r
berth	la couchette	koo-shet
beside	à côté de	a koh-tay de^r
best	le meilleur/la meilleure	may-œr/may-œr
bet	le pari	pa-ree
better	mieux/meilleur	myœ/may-œr
between	entre	ah^{n}tr
bicycle	la bicyclette/le vélo	bee-see-klet/ve-loh
big	grand	grah^n
bill	la note/l'addition f	not/la-dee-syoh^n
binoculars	les jumelles f	zhu^e-mel

bird	l'oiseau *m*	lwa-zoh
birthday	l'anniversaire *m*	la-nee-vair-sair
bit	le morceau	mor-soh
bite (to) *insect*	piquer	pee-kay
bite (to) *animal*	mordre	mor-dr
bitter	amer	a-mair
blanket	la couverture	koo-vair-tu^{e}r
bleed (to)	saigner	sen-yay
blind	aveugle	a-vœgl
blond	blond	bloh^n
blood	le sang	sah^n
blouse	le chemisier	she^r-mee-zyay
blow	le coup	koo
blow (to)	souffler	soo-flay
on board	à bord	a bor
boarding house	la pension	pah^n-syoh^n
boat	le bateau/la barque	bat-oh/bark
body	le corps	kor
bolt	le verrou	ve-roo
bone	l'os *m*	los
bonfire	le feu (de joie)	fœ
book	le livre	leevr
book (to)	réserver/louer	ray-sair-vay/loo-ay

boot	la botte/la chaussure montante	bot/shoh-su^{e}r mohn-tahnt
border	la frontière	frohn-tyair
borrow (to)	emprunter	ahn-pren-tay
both	(tous) les deux	too lay de^r
bottle	la bouteille	boo-te-y
bottle opener	l'ouvre-bouteille *m*	loovr-boo-te-y
bottom	le fond	fohn
bowl	le bol	bol
box *container*	la boîte	bwat
box *theatre*	la loge	lozh
box office	le bureau de location	bu^e-roh de^r lo-ka-syohn
boy	le garçon	gar-sohn
bracelet	le bracelet	bra-slay
braces	les bretelles *f*	bre^r-tel
brain	le cerveau	sair-voh
branch *tree*	la branche	brahnsh
branch *office*	la succursale	su^e-ku^{e}r-sal
brand	la marque	mark
brassière	le soutien-gorge	soo-tyan gorzh
break (to)	casser	ka-say
breakfast	le petit déjeuner	pe^r-tee day-zhe^r-nay
breathe (to)	respirer	res-peer-ay

bridge	le pont	poh^n
briefs	le slip	sleep
bright	brillant	bree-yah^n
bring (to)	apporter	a-por-tay
British	britannique	bree-tan-eek
broken	cassé	kas-ay
brooch	la broche	brosh
brother	le frère	frair
bruise (to)	contusionner	koh^n-tu^e-zyo-nay
brush	la brosse	bros
brush (to)	brosser	bro-say
bucket	le seau	soh
buckle	la boucle	bookl
build (to)	construire	kon-strweer
building	le bâtiment	ba-tee-mah^n
bunch *flowers*	le bouquet	boo-kay
bunch *keys*	le trousseau	troo-soh
buoy	la bouée	boo-ay
burn (to)	brûler	bru^e-lay
burst (to)	éclater/crever	ay-kla-tay/kre^r-vay
bus	l'autobus *m*	loh-toh-bu^es
bus stop	l'arrêt *m*	la-re
business	l'affaire *f*	la-fair
busy	occupé	ok-u^e-pay

but	mais	me
button	le bouton	boo-tohⁿ
buy (to)	acheter	ash-tay
by *near*	près (de)	pre (de^r)
by *via, means*	par	par

C

cab	le taxi	tak-see
cabin	la cabine	ka-been
call	l'appel *m*	la-pel
call *telephone*	le coup de téléphone	koo de^r tay-lay-fon
call *visit*	la visite	vee-zeet
call (to) *summon, name*	appeler	ap-lay
call (to) *telephone*	téléphoner	tay-lay-fo-nay
call on, at (to)	rendre visite à	rahⁿdr vee-zeet a
calm	calme	kalm
camp (to)	camper	kahⁿ-pay
camp site	le terrain de camping	te-raⁿ de^r kahⁿ-ping
can (to be able)	pouvoir	poo-vwar
can *tin*	la boîte	bwat
Canada	le Canada	ka-na-da
Canadian	canadien/canadienne	ka-na-dyaⁿ (-dyen)
cancel (to)	annuler	anu^e-lay

candle	la bougie	boo-zhee
canoe	le canoë	ka-noh-ay
cap	la casquette	kas-ket
capable	capable	ka-pabl
capital city	la capitale	ka-pee-tal
car	l'auto *f*/la voiture	loh-toh/vwa-tu^{e}r
car park	le parking	par-king
	le parc de stationnement	park de^r sta-syon-mah^n
caravan	la caravane	karavan
card	la carte	kart
care	le soin	swa^n
careful	soigneux/prudent	swan-ye^r/pru^{e}dah^n
careless	négligent	nay-glee-zhah^n
carry (to)	porter	por-tay
cash	l'argent *m*	lar-zhah^n
cash (to)	encaisser	ah^n-kes-ay
cashier	le caissier/la caissière	kes-yay (-yair)
casino	le casino	ka-zee-noh
castle	le château	sha-toh
cat	le chat	sha
catalogue	le catalogue	ka-ta-log
catch (to)	attraper	atrap-ay
cathedral	la cathédrale	ka-tay-dral

catholic	catholique	ka-toh-leek
cause	la cause	kohz
cave	la caverne/la grotte	ka-vairn/grot
central	central	sah^n-tral
centre	le centre	sah^{n}tr
century	le siècle	sy-ekl
ceremony	la cérémonie	say-ray-mon-ee
certain	certain	sair-ta^n
certainly	certainement	sair-ten-mah^n
chair	la chaise	shez
chambermaid	la femme de chambre	fam de^r shah^n-br
chance	le hasard/la chance	a-zar/shah^{n}s
(small) change	la monnaie	mo-nay
change (to)	changer	shah^n-zhay
charge	le prix	pree
charge (to)	demander (un prix)	de^r-mah^n-day (un pree)
cheap	bon marché	boh^n mar-shay
check (to)	vérifier	vay-reef-yay
cheque	le chèque	shek
child	l'enfant *m* or *f*	lah^n-fah^n
china	la porcelaine	pors-len
choice	le choix	shwa
choose (to)	choisir	shwa-zeer
church	l'église *f*	lay-gleez

cigarette case	l'étui à cigarettes *m*	lay-twee a see-gar-et
cinema	le cinéma	see-nay-ma
circle *theatre*	le balcon	bal-kohⁿ
circus	le cirque	seerk
city	la grande ville	grahⁿd veel
class	la classe	klas
clean	propre	propr
clean (to)	nettoyer	ne-twa-yay
clear	clair	klair
clerk	l'employé(e) *m* or *f*	ahⁿ-plwa-yay
cliff	la falaise	fa-lez
climb (to)	monter	mohⁿ-tay
cloakroom	le vestiaire	ves-tyair
clock	la pendule/l'horloge *f*	pahⁿ-du^el/lor-lozh
close (to)	fermer	fair-may
closed	fermé	fair-may
cloth	l'étoffe *f*	lay-tof
clothes	les vêtements *m*	vet-mahⁿ
cloud	le nuage	nu^e-azh
coach	l'autocar *m*	loh-toh-kar
coast	la côte	koht
coat	le manteau	mahⁿ-toh
coat hanger	le cintre	saⁿtr
coin	la pièce de monnaie	pyes de^r mo-nay

cold	froid	frwa
collar	le col	kol
collar stud	le bouton de col	boo-toh^n de^r kol
collect (to)	collectionner	ko-lek-syo-nay
colour	la couleur	koo-lœr
comb	le peigne	pen-y
come (to)	venir	ve^r-neer
come in!	entrez!	ah^n-tray
comfortable	confortable	koh^n-for-tabl
common	ordinaire/commun	or-dee-nair/ko-me^n
company	la compagnie/la société	koh^n-pan-yee/so-syay-tay
compartment	le compartiment	koh^n-par-tee-mah^n
complain (to)	se plaindre (de)	se^r pla^{n}dr (de^r)
complaint	la plainte	pla^{n}t
completely	complètement	koh^n-plet-mah^n
concert	le concert	koh^n-sair
condition	la condition	koh^n-dee-syoh^n
conductor *bus*	le receveur	re^r-se^r-vœr
conductor *orchestra*	le chef d'orchestre	shef dor-kestr
congratulations!	félicitations!	fay-lee-see-ta-syoh^n
connect (to)	relier/(*train*) faire la correspondance avec	re^r-lee-ay/fair la ko-res-poh^n-dah^{n}s a-vek
connection	la correspondance	ko-res-poh^n-dah^{n}s

consul	le consul	koh^n-su^{e}l
consulate	le consulat	koh^n-su^e-la
contain (to)	contenir	koh^n-te^r-neer
contrast	le contraste	koh^n-trast
convenient	commode	ko-mod
conversation	la conversation	koh^n-vair-sa-syoh^n
cook	le cuisinier/la cuisinière	kwee-zee-nyay (-nyair)
cook (to)	cuire	kweer
cool	frais	fre
copper	le cuivre	kweevr
copy *book*	l'exemplaire *m*	eg-zah^n-plair
copy *duplicate*	la copie	ko-pee
copy (to)	copier	ko-pyay
cork	le bouchon	boo-shoh^n
corkscrew	le tire-bouchon	teer boo-shoh^n
corner	le coin	kwa^n
correct	exact	egzakt
corridor	le couloir	kool-war
cosmetics	les produits de beauté *m*	pro-dwee de^r boh-tay
cost	le prix	pree
cost (to)	coûter	koo-tay
cot	le petit lit	pe^r-tee lee

cottage	la villa	vee-la
cotton	le coton	ko-toh^n
cotton wool	le coton hydrophile	ko-toh^n eedro-feel
couchette	la couchette	koo-shet
count (to)	compter	koh^n-tay
country *nation*	le pays	pay-ee
country *not town*	la campagne	kah^n-pan-y
couple	le couple	koopl
course *dish*	le plat	pla
courtyard	la cour	koor
cousin	le cousin/la cousine	koo-za^n (-zeen)
cover	la couverture	koo-vair-tu^{e}r
cover (to)	couvrir	koo-vreer
cover charge	le couvert	koo-vair
cow	la vache	vash
credit	le crédit	kray-dee
crew	l'équipage *m*	lay-kee-pazh
cross	la croix	krwa
cross (to)	traverser	tra-vair-say
crossroads	le croisement	krwaz-mah^n
crowd	la foule	fool
crowded	plein de monde	pla^n de^r moh^{n}d
cry (to) *shout*	crier	kree-ay
cry (to) *weep*	pleurer	plœ-ray

cufflinks	les boutons de manchette	boo-tohⁿ de^r mahⁿ-shet
cup	la tasse	tas
cupboard	le placard/l'armoire *f*	pla-kar/lar-mwar
cure (to)	guérir	gay-reer
curious	curieux	ku^e-rye^r
curl	la boucle	bookl
current	le courant	koo-rahⁿ
curtain	le rideau	ree-doh
curve	la courbe	koorb
cushion	le coussin	koo-saⁿ
customs	la douane	dwan
customs officer	le douanier	dwan-yay
cut	la coupure	koo-pu^er
cut (to)	couper	koo-pay

D

daily	tous les jours	too lay zhoor
damaged	endommagé	ahⁿ-dom-azh-ay
damp	humide	u^em-eed
dance	la danse/le bal	dahⁿs/bal
dance (to)	danser	dahⁿ-say
danger	le danger	dahⁿ-zhay

dangerous	dangereux	dahn-zher-rer
dark	noir/obscur	nwar/op-skuer
dark *colour*	foncé	fohn-say
date *appointment*	le rendez-vous	rahn-day voo
date *time*	la date	dat
daughter	la fille	fee-y
day	le jour/la journée	zhoor/zhoor-nay
dead	mort	mor
deaf	sourd	soor
dear	cher	shair
decide (to)	décider	day-see-day
deck	le pont	pohn
deckchair	la chaise longue	shez long
declare (to)	déclarer	day-klar-ay
deep	profond	pro-fohn
delay	le retard	rer-tar
deliver (to)	livrer	lee-vray
delivery	la livraison	lee-vrai-zohn
demi-pension	la demi-pension	der-mee pahn-syohn
dentures	le dentier	dahn-tyay
deodorant	le désodorisant	day-zo-dor-ee-zahn
depart (to)	partir	par-teer
department	le département	day-par-ter-mahn
department store	le grand magasin	grahn ma-ga-zan

departure	le départ	day-par
dessert	le dessert	de-ser
detour	le détour	day-toor
dial (to)	faire un numéro	fair en nue-may-roh
diamond	le diamant	dya-mahn
dice	le dé	day
dictionary	le dictionnaire	deek-syon-air
diet	le régime	ray-zheem
diet (to)	être au régime	etr oh ray-zheem
different	différent	dee-fay-rahn
difficult	difficile	dee-fee-seel
dine (to)	dîner	dee-nay
dining room	la salle à manger	sal a mahn-zhay
dinner	le dîner	dee-nay
direct	direct	dee-rekt
direction	la direction	dee-rek-syohn
dirty	sale	sal
disappointed	déçu	day-sue
discothèque	la discothèque	dees-koh-tek
dish	le plat	pla
disinfectant	le désinfectant	day-zan-fek-tahn
distance	la distance	dee-stahns
disturb (to)	déranger	day-rahn-zhay
ditch	le fossé	fo-say

dive (to)	plonger	plohⁿ-zhay
diving board	le plongeoir	plohⁿ-zhwar
divorced	divorcé(e)	dee-vor-say
do (to)	faire	fair
dock (to)	accoster	akost-ay
doctor	le médecin	mayd-saⁿ
dog	le chien	shyaⁿ
doll	la poupée	poo-pay
door	la porte	port
double	double	doobl
double bed	le grand lit	grahⁿ lee
double room	la chambre pour deux	shahⁿbr poor deʳ
down (stairs)	en bas	ahⁿ ba
dozen	la douzaine	doo-zen
drawer	le tiroir	teer-war
dream	le rêve	rev
dress	la robe	rob
dressing gown	la robe de chambre	rob deʳ shahⁿbr
dressmaker	le couturier/la couturière	koo-tuʳ-yay (-yair)
drink (to)	boire	bwar
drinking water	l'eau potable *f*	loh pot-abl
drive (to)	conduire	kohⁿ-dweer
driver	le chauffeur	shoh-fœr

drop (to)	faire tomber	fair tohⁿ-bay
drunk *adj*	ivre	eevr
drunk *noun*	l'ivrogne	lee-vron-y
dry	sec	sek
during	pendant	pahⁿ-dahⁿ

E

each	chaque	shak
early	tôt/de bonne heure	toh/de^r bon œr
earrings	les boucles d'oreilles *f*	bookl dor-ay
east	l'est *m*	lest
easy	facile	fa-seel
eat (to)	manger	mahⁿ-zhay
edge	le bord	bor
eiderdown	l'édredon *m*	lay-dre^r-dohⁿ
elastic	l'élastique *m*	lay-las-teek
electric light bulb	l'ampoule *f*	lahⁿ-pool
electric point	la prise de courant	preez de^r koo-rahⁿ
electricity	l'électricité *f*	ay-lek-tree-see-tay
elevator	l'ascenseur *m*	la-sahⁿ-sœr
embarrassed	gêné	zhe-nay
embassy	l'ambassade *f*	lahⁿ-ba-sad
emergency exit	la sortie de secours	sor-tee de^r se^r-koor

empty	vide	veed
end	la fin	faⁿ
engaged *people*	fiancé(e)	fyahⁿ-say
engaged *telephone*	occupé	o-kuᵉ-pay
engine	le moteur	moh-tœr
England	l'Angleterre *f*	lahⁿ-glerᵉ-tair
English	anglais/anglaise	ahⁿ-gle (-glez)
enjoy (to)	aimer	e-may
enjoy oneself (to)	s'amuser	sa-muᵉ-zay
enough	assez	asay
enquiries	les renseignements *m*	rahⁿ-sen-yerᵉ-mahⁿ
enter (to)	entrer	ahⁿ-tray
entrance	l'entrée *f*	lahⁿ-tray
envelope	l'enveloppe *f*	lahⁿ-vlop
equipment	l'équipement *m*	lay-keep-mahⁿ
escape (to)	s'échapper	say-sha-pay
Europe	l'Europe *f*	lœr-op
even *opp. odd*	pair	pair
event	l'événement *m*	lay-vay-nerᵉ-mahⁿ
every	chaque	shak
everybody	tout le monde	too lerᵉ mohⁿd
everything	tout	too
everywhere	partout	par-too
example	l'exemple *m*	leg-zahⁿpl

excellent	excellent	ek-se-lahⁿ
except	sauf/excepté	sohf/ek-sep-tay
excess	l'excédent *m*	lek-say-dahⁿ
exchange bureau	le bureau de change	bu^e-roh de^r shanzh
exchange rate	le taux (du change)	toh
excursion	l'excursion *f*	lek-sku^er-syohⁿ
excuse	l'excuse *f*	lek-su^ez
exhausted	épuisé	ay-pwee-zay
exhibition	l'exposition *f*	lek-spo-zee-syohⁿ
exit	la sortie	sor-tee
expect (to) *someone*	attendre	at-ahⁿdr
expensive	cher	shair
explain (to)	expliquer	ek-splee-kay
express *letter*	exprès	ek-spres
express train	l'express *m*	lek-spres
extra	supplémentaire	su^e-play-mahⁿ-tair
eye shadow	l'ombre à paupières *f*	lohⁿbr a poh-pyair

F

fabric	le tissu	tee-su^e
face	le visage/la figure	ve-zazh/fee-gu^er
face cream	la crème de beauté	krem de^r boh-tay
face powder	la poudre de riz	poodr de^r ree

fact	le fait	fe
factory	la fabrique/l'usine *f*	fab-reek/lu^e-zeen
fade (to)	se faner	se^r fa-nay
faint (to)	s'évanouir	say-van-weer
fair	blond	bloh^n
fair *fête*	la foire	fwar
fall (to)	tomber	toh^n-bay
family	la famille	fa-mee-y
far	loin	lwa^n
fare	le prix du billet	pree du^e bee-yay
farm	la ferme	fairm
farmer	le fermier	fair-myay
farther	plus loin	plu^e lwa^n
fashion	la mode	mod
fast	vite	veet
fat	gras	gra
father	le père	pair
fault	le défaut	day-foh
fear	la peur	pœr
feed (to)	nourrir	noo-reer
feel (to)	sentir	sah^n-teer
female *adj*	féminin	fay-mee-na^n
ferry	le ferry	fe-ree
fetch (to)	apporter	a-por-tay

few	peu	pe[r]
fiancé(e)	le fiancé/la fiancée	fyah[n]-say
field	le champ	shah[n]
fight (to)	se battre	se[r] battre
fill (to)	remplir	rah[n]-pleer
film	le film	feelm
find (to)	trouver	troo-vay
fine	beau	boh
finish (to)	finir	fee-neer
finished	fini	fee-nee
fire	le feu	fœ
fire escape	l'issu de secours *f*	eesu[e] de[r] se[r]-koor
first	premier	pre[r]m-yay
first aid	les premiers secours *m*	pre[r]m-yay se[r]-koor
first class *noun*	la première classe	pre[r]m-yair klas
fish	le poisson	pwa-soh[n]
fish (to)	pêcher	pe-shay
fisherman	le pêcheur	pe-shœr
fit *adj*	en forme	ah[n] form
fit (to)	aller bien	a-lay by-a[n]
flag	le drapeau	dra-poh
flat *adj*	plat	pla
flat *noun*	l'appartement *m*	la-par-te[r]-mah[n]
flight	le vol	vol

float (to)	flotter	floh-tay
flood	l'inondation *f*	lee-nohⁿ-da-syohⁿ
floor	le plancher	plahⁿ-shay
floor *storey*	l'étage *m*	lay-tazh
floor show	le spectacle	spek-takl
flower	la fleur	flœr
fly	la mouche	moosh
fly (to)	voler	vo-lay
fly (to) *in plane*	aller en avion	a-lay ahⁿ av-yohⁿ
fog	le brouillard	brwee-yar
fold (to)	plier	plee-yay
follow (to)	suivre	sweevr
food	la nourriture	noo-ree-tu^er
foot	le pied	pyay
football	le football	foot-bal
footpath	le sentier	sahⁿ-tyay
for	pour	poor
foreign	étranger	ay-trahⁿ-zhay
forest	la forêt	for-ay
forget (to)	oublier	oob-ly-ay
fork	la fourchette	foor-shet
forward	en avant	on avahⁿ
forward (to)	faire suivre	fair sweevr
fountain	la fontaine	fon-ten

fragile	fragile	fra-zheel
France	la France	frah^{n}s
free	libre	leebr
freight	le fret	fre
French	français/française	frah^n-say (-sez)
fresh	frais	fre
fresh water	l'eau douce *f*	loh doos
friend	l'ami *m*/l'amie *f*	la-mee
friendly	amical	a-mee-kal
from	de	de^r
front	le devant	de^{r}vah^n
frontier	la frontière	froh^n-tyair
frozen	gelé	zhe^r-lay
frozen *food*	congelé/surgelé	koh^n-zhe^r-lay/su^{e}r-zhe^r-lay
fruit	le fruit	frwee
full	plein	pla^n
full board	la pension complète	pah^n-syoh^n kom-plet
fun	l'amusement *m*	a-mu^e-se^r-mah^n
funny	drôle	drohl
fur	la fourrure	foo-ru^{e}r
furniture	les meubles *m*	mœbl
further	plus loin	plu^e lwa^n

G

gallery	la galerie	gal-ree
gamble (to)	jouer (de l'argent)	zhoo-ay (de^r lar-zhah^n)
game	la partie	par-tee
garage	le garage	ga-razh
garbage	les ordures *f*	ordu^{e}r
garden	le jardin	zhar-da^n
gas	le gaz	gaz
gate	la porte/le portail	port/por-ta-y
gentleman	monsieur	me^r-sye^r
gentlemen	les toilettes (messieurs)	twa-let (mes-ye^r)
get (to)	obtenir	ob-te^r-neer
get off (to)	descendre	de-sah^{n}dr
get on (to)	monter	moh^n-tay
gift	le cadeau	ka-doh
girdle	la gaine	ghen
girl	la jeune fille	zhœn fee-y
give (to)	donner	don-ay
glad	heureux	œr-e^r
glass	le verre	vair
glasses	les lunettes *f*	lu^e-nett
gloomy	sombre	soh^{n}br

glorious	splendide	splahⁿ-deed
glove	le gant	gahⁿ
go (to)	aller	alay
goal	le but	bu^e
god	Dieu	dye^r
gold	l'or *m*	lor
good	bon	bohⁿ
government	le gouvernement	goo-vair-ne^r-mahⁿ
granddaughter	la petite-fille	pe^r-teet fee-y
grandfather	le grand-père	grahⁿ pair
grandmother	la grand-mère	grahⁿ mair
grandson	le petit-fils	pe^r-tee fees
grass	l'herbe *f*	lerb
grateful	reconnaissant	ree-ko-ne-sahⁿ
gravel	le gravier	gra-vyay
great	grand	grahⁿ
groceries	les comestibles *m*	ko-mes-teebl
ground	le sol	sol
grow (to)	grandir	grahⁿ-deer
grow (to) *plants*	pousser	poo-say
guarantee	la garantie	gar-ahⁿ-tee
guard	le garde	gard
guard *on train*	le chef de train	shef de^r traⁿ
guest	l'invité	laⁿ-vee-tay

| guide *book, person* | le guide | gheed |

H

hail	la grêle	grel
hair	les cheveux *m*	sher-ver
hair brush	la brosse à cheveux	bros a sher-ver
hairgrip	la barrette	ba-ret
hairpin	l'épingle	lay-pangl
half	demi	der-mee
half-board	la demi-pension	der-mee pahn-syohn
half fare	une place à demi-tarif	plas a der-mee ta-reef
hammer	le marteau	mar-toh
hand	la main	man
handbag	le sac à main	sak a man
handkerchief	le mouchoir	moo-shwar
hang (to)	pendre	pahndr
hanger	le cintre	santr
happen (to)	arriver	ar-ee-vay
happy	heureux	œr-er
happy birthday	bon anniversaire	bon a-nee-vair-sair
harbour	le port	por
hard	dur/difficile	duer/dee-fee-seel

hardly	à peine	a pen
hat	le chapeau	sha-poh
have (to)	avoir	avwar
he	il	eel
head	la tête	tet
health	la santé	sah^n-tay
hear (to)	entendre	ah^n-tah^n-dr
heart	le cœur	kœr
heat	la chaleur	sha-lœr
heating	le chauffage	shoh-fazh
heavy	lourd	loor
heel *foot, shoe*	le talon	tal-oh^n
height	la hauteur	oh-tœr
help	l'aide *f*	led
help (to)	aider	ed-ay
hem	l'ourlet *m*	loor-lay
her/his	son *m*/sa *f*/ses *pl*	soh^n/sa/say
here	ici	ee-see
hers/his	la sienne/le sien	syen/sya^n
high	haut	oh
hike (to)	faire une excursion (à pied)	fair u^n ek-scu^{er}-zy-oh^n a pyay
hill	la colline	kol-een
him	lui/le	lwee/le^r

hire (to)	louer	loo-ay
his/her	son *m*/sa *f*/ses *pl*	sohn/sa/say
his/hers	le sien/la sienne	syan/syen
hitch hike (to)	faire de l'auto-stop	fair de loh-toh stop
hold (to)	tenir	te-neer
hole	le trou	troo
holiday	le jour férié	zhoor fay-ryay
holidays	les vacances *f*	vak-ahns
hollow	creux	krer
(at) home	chez soi/à la maison	shay swa/a la me-zohn
honeymoon	la lune de miel	luen der myel
hope	l'espoir *m*	les-pwar
hope (to)	espérer	es-pay-ray
horse	le cheval	sher-val
horse race	la course de chevaux	koors de sher-voh
horse riding	l'équitation	lay-kee-ta-syohn
hospital	l'hôpital *m*	lop-ee-tal
host/hostess	l'hôte *m*/l'hôtesse *f*	loht/lohtes
hot	chaud	shoh
hot water bottle	la bouillotte	boo-yot
hotel	l'hôtel *m*	loh-tel
hotel keeper	l'hôtelier	loh-tel-yay
hour	l'heure *f*	loer
house	la maison	me-zohn

how?	comment	ko-mah^n
how much/many?	combien	koh^n-bya^n
hungry (to be)	(avoir) faim	avwar fa^n
hurry (to)	se dépêcher	se day-pesh-ay
hurt (to)	faire mal	fair mal
husband	le mari	ma-ree

I

I	je	zhe^r
if	si	see
immediately	immédiatement	ee-may-dyat-mah^n
important	important	a^n-por-tah^n
in	dans	dah^n
include (to)	comprendre	koh^n-prah^{n}dr
included	compris	koh^n-pree
inconvenient	inopportun	een-op-or-te^n
incorrect	inexact	een-egzakt
indeed	vraiment	vre-mah^n
indoors	à l'intérieur	a la^n-tay-ryαr
information	les renseignements *m*	rah^n-sen-y-mah^n
information bureau	le bureau de renseignements	bue-roh de^r rah^n-sen-y-mah^n
ink	l'encre *f*	lah^{n}kr

inn	l'auberge *f*	loh-bairzh
insect	l'insecte *m*	lan-sekt
insect bite	la piqûre (d'insecte)	pee-kuer
insect repellant	le produit pour	pro-dwee poor
	éloigner les insectes	ay-lwan-yay lay
		zan-sekt
inside	à l'intérieur	a lan-tay-ryœr
instead (of)	au lieu (de)	oh lyer der
instructor	l'instructeur *m*	lan-struek-tœr
insurance	l'assurance *f*	la-suer-ahns
insure (to)	assurer	as-uer-ay
interested	intéressé	an-tay-re-say
interesting	intéressant	an-tay-res-ahn
interpreter	l'interprète *m*	lan-tair-pret
into	dans	dahn
introduce (to)	présenter	pray-zahn-tay
invitation	l'invitation *f*	lan-vee-ta-syohn
invite (to)	inviter	an-vee-tay
Ireland	l'Irlande *f*	leer-lahnd
Irish	irlandais/irlandaise	eer-lahn-de (-dez)
iron (to)	repasser	rer-pas-ay
island	l'île *f*	leel
it	il/elle	eel/el

J

jacket	la veste	vest
jar	le pot	poh
jelly fish	la méduse	may-du^{e}z
jewellery	la bijouterie	bee-zhoo-tree
job	l'emploi *m*/le travail	lah^n-plwa/tra-vy
journey	le voyage	vwa-yazh
jump (to)	sauter	soh-tay
jumper	le pull(over)	pu^{e}l(ovair)

K

keep (to)	garder/tenir	gar-day/te^r-neer
key	la clé	klay
kind	l'espèce *f*/la sorte	les-pes/sort
kind *adj*	aimable/gentil	emable/zhah^n-tee
king	le roi	rwa
kiss	le baiser	be-zay
kiss (to)	embrasser	ah^n-bra-say
kitchen	la cuisine	kwee-zeen
knickers/briefs	la culotte/le slip	ku^e-lot/sleep
knife	le couteau	koo-toh

knock (to)	frapper	fra-pay
know (to) *a fact*	savoir	sa-vwar
know (to) *a person*	connaître	kon-etr

l

label	l'étiquette *f*	lay-tee-ket
lace	la dentelle	dahⁿ-tel
ladies	les toilettes (dames) *f*	twa-let (dam)
lady	la dame	dam
lake	le lac	lak
lake *ornamental*	le bassin	ba-saⁿ
lamp	la lampe	lahⁿp
land	la terre	ter
landing	le palier	pal-yay
landlord/lady	le/la propriétaire	prop-ree-ay-tair
lane	le chemin	she^r-maⁿ
language	la langue	lahⁿg
large	grand	grahⁿ
last	dernier	dair-nyay
late	tard/en retard	tar/ahⁿ re^r-tar
laugh (to)	rire	reer
lavatory	les toilettes *f*	twa-let
lavatory paper	le papier hygiénique	pap-yay ee-zhay-neek

law	la loi	lwa
lead (to)	conduire	koh^n-dweer
leaf	la feuille	foe-y
leak (to)	perdre	pairdr
learn (to)	apprendre	ap-rah^ndr
least	le moins	mwa^n
at least	au moins	oh mwa^n
leather	le cuir	kweer
leave (to) *abandon*	quitter	kee-tay
leave (to) *go away*	partir	par-teer
left *opp. right*	gauche	gohsh
left luggage	la consigne	koh^n-seen-y
leg	la jambe	zhah^nb
lend (to)	prêter	pre-tay
length	la longueur	loh^n-gœr
less	moins	mwa^n
lesson	la leçon	le^r-soh^n
let (to) *rent*	louer	loo-ay
let (to) *allow*	laisser/permettre	le-say/pair-metr
letter	la lettre	letr
level crossing	le passage à niveau	pa-sazh a nee-voh
library	la bibliothèque	bee-blyoh-tek
licence	le permis	pair-mee
life	la vie	vee

lift	l'ascenseur *m*	la-sahⁿ-sœr
light *colour*	clair	klair
light *weight*	léger	lay-zhay
light	la lumière	lu^em-yair
lighter fuel	l'essence à briquet	gaz/les-ahⁿs a bree-kay
lighthouse	le phare	far
like (to)	aimer	emay
line	la ligne	leen-y
linen	le linge	laⁿzh
lingerie	la lingerie	laⁿzh-ree
lipstick	le rouge à lèvres	roozh a levr
liquid *adj*	liquide	lee-keed
liquid *noun*	le liquide	lee-keed
listen (to)	écouter	ay-koo-tay
little *size*	petit	pe^r-tee
little *amount*	peu	pe^r
live (to)	vivre	veevr
local	local	lo-kal
lock	la serrure	ser-u^er
lock (to)	fermer à clé	fair-may a klay
long	long/longue	lohⁿ/lohⁿg
look (to) *at*	regarder	re^r-gar-day
look (to) *like*	ressembler	re^r-sahⁿ-blay
look (to) *for*	chercher	shair-shay

loose	lâche/desserré	lash/de-se-ray
lorry	le camion	ka-myoh^n
lose (to)	perdre	pairdr
lost property office	les objets trouvés *m*	lay zob-zhay troo-vay
lot	beaucoup	boh-koo
loud	bruyant	brwee-ah^n
love (to)	aimer	e-may
lovely	beau/belle	boh/bel
low	bas	ba
luggage	les bagages *m*	bag-azh
(piece of) luggage	le colis	ko-lee
lunch	le déjeuner	day-zhe^r-nay

M

mad	fou/folle	foo/fol
magazine	la revue/le magazine	re^r-vu^e/ma-ga-zeen
maid	la domestique	dom-est-eek
mail	le courrier	koor-yay
main street	la rue principale	ru^e pra^n-see-pal
make (to)	faire	fair
make love (to)	faire l'amour	fair la-moor
make-up	le maquillage	ma-kee-yazh
male *adj*	masculin	mas-kue-la^n

man	l'homme *m*	lom
manage (to)	se débrouiller	se^r day-brwee-yay
manager	le directeur/le patron	dee-rek-tœr/pat-rohⁿ
manicure	le manucure	ma-nu^e-ku^er
many	beaucoup (de)	boh-koo (de^r)
map *country*	la carte	kart
map *town*	le plan	plahⁿ
marble	le marbre	marbr
market	le marché	mar-shay
market place	la place du marché	plas du^e mar-shay
married	marié	mar-yay
Mass	la messe	mes
massage	le massage	mas-azh
match *light*	l'allumette *f*	lal-u^emet
match *sport*	le match	match
material	le tissu	tee-su^e
matinée	la matinée	ma-tee-nay
mattress	le matelas	mat-la
maybe	peut-être	pe^r-tetr
me	moi	mwa
meal	le repas	re^r-pa
measurements	les mesures *f*	me^r-zu^er
meet (to)	rencontrer	rahⁿ-kohⁿ-tray
mend (to)	réparer	ray-pa-ray

mess	le désordre	day-zordr
message	le message	mes-azh
metal	le métal	may-tal
middle	le milieu	meel-yœ
middle-aged	d'âge mûr	dazh muᵉr
middle class *noun*	la classe moyenne	klas mwa-yen
mild	doux	doo
mine	le mien/la mienne	myaⁿ/myen
minute	la minute	mee-nuᵉt
mirror	le miroir	meer-war
Miss	Mademoiselle (Mlle)	mad-mwa-zel
miss (to)	manquer	mahⁿ-kay
mistake	l'erreur *f*	ler-œr
mix (to)	mélanger	may-lahⁿ-zhay
mixed	mélangé	may-lahⁿ-zhay
modern	moderne	mod-airn
moment	le moment	mo-mahⁿ
money	l'argent *m*	lar-zhahⁿ
month	le mois	mwa
monument	le monument	mo-nuᵉ-mahⁿ
moon	la lune	luᵉn
more	plus/davantage (de)	pluᵉ/dav-ahⁿ-tazh
mosquito	le moustique	moo-steek
most	la plupart	pluᵉ-par

mother	la mère	mair
motor boat	le canot à moteur	kan-oh a moh-tœr
motor cycle	la motocyclette	moh-toh-see-klet
motor racing	la course automobile	koors oh-toh-moh-beel
motorway	l'autoroute *f*	loh-toh-root
mountain	la montagne	moh^n-tan-y
mouth	la bouche	boosh
mouthwash	l'eau dentifrice	loh dah^n-tee-frees
move (to)	bouger/remuer	boo-zhay/re^r-mu^e-ay
Mr	Monsieur (M.)	me^r-sye^r
Mrs	Madame (Mme)	ma-dam
much	beaucoup (de)	boh-koo
museum	le musée	mu^e-zay
music	la musique	mu^e-zeek
must (to have to)	devoir	de^r-vwar
my	mon *m*/ma *f*/mes *pl*	moh^n/ma/may
myself	moi-même	mwa-mem

N

nail	le clou	kloo
nail polish	le vernis à ongles	vair-nee a oh^n-gl
nailbrush	la brosse à ongles	bros a oh^n-gl
nailfile	la lime à ongles	leem a oh^n-gl

name	le nom	noh^n
napkin	la serviette	sair-vyet
nappy	la couche	koosh
narrow	étroit	ay-trwa
near	près (de)	pre
nearly	presque	presk
necessary	nécessaire	nay-ses-air
necklace	le collier	kol-yay
need (to)	avoir besoin (de)	avwar be^r-zwa^n
needle	l'aiguille *f*	leg-weey
net	le filet	fee-lay
never	jamais	zha-me
new *brand new*	neuf/neuve	nœf/nœv
new *fresh, latest*	nouveau/nouvelle	noo-voh/noo-vel
news	les nouvelles *f*	noo-vel
newspaper	le journal	zhoor-nal
next	prochain/suivant	pro-sha^n/swee-vah^n
nice	gentil	zhah^n-tee
nightclub	la boîte de nuit	bwat de^r nwee
nightdress	la chemise de nuit	she^r-meez de^r nwee
nobody	personne	pair-son
noisy	bruyant	brwee-ah^n
none	aucun	oh-ke^n

north	le nord	nor
not	ne . . . pas	ne^r . . . pa
note *money*	le billet	bee-yay
notebook	le carnet/le cahier	kar-nay/ka-yay
nothing	rien	ry-a^n
notice	l'avis *m*	la-vee
notice (to)	remarquer	re^r-mar-kay
novel	le roman	ro-mah^n
now	maintenant	ma^n-te^r-nah^n
number	le numéro	nu^e-may-roh
nylon	le nylon	nee-loh^n
nylons	les bas nylon *m*	ba nee-loh^n

O

occasion	l'occasion *f*	lo-ka-zyoh^n
occupation	le métier	may-tyay
occupied	occupé	ok-u^{e}pay
ocean	l'océan *m*	lo-say-ah^n
odd *opp. even*	impair	a^n-pair
odd *strange*	singulier	sa^n-gu^e-lyay
of	de	de^r
offer	l'offre *f*	loffr
offer (to)	offrir	off-reer

office	le bureau	bu^e-roh
officer	l'officier *m*	lo-fee-syay
official *adj*	officiel	of-ee-syel
official *noun*	l'employé/le fonctionnaire	lahⁿ-plwa-yay/fohⁿk-syo-nair
often	souvent	soo-vahⁿ
oily	gras	gra
ointment	la pommade	po-mad
old	vieux/vieille	vye^r/vyay
on	sur	su^er
once	une fois	fwa
only *adj/adv*	seul/seulement	sœl/sœl-mahⁿ
open *pp*	ouvert	oo-vair
open (to)	ouvrir	oo-vreer
opening	l'ouverture	loo-vair-tu^er
opera	l'opéra *m*	lop-ay-ra
opportunity	l'occasion *f*	lo-ka-zyohⁿ
opposite	en face (de)	ahⁿ fas
or	ou	oo
orchestra	l'orchestre *m*	lor-kestr
order (to)	commander	ko-mahⁿ-day
ordinary	ordinaire	or-dee-nair
other	autre	ohtr
otherwise	autrement	oh-tre^r-mahⁿ

ought	devoir	deʳ-vwar
our	notre s/nos pl	notr/noh
ours	le/la nôtre	nohtr
out of order	en panne/détraqué	ahⁿ pan/day-trak-ay
outside	dehors	deʳ-or
over	au-dessus (de)	oh-deʳ-sueᵉ
over *finished*	fini	fee-nee
overcoat	le pardessus	par-deʳ-sueᵉ
overnight	pour la nuit	poor la nwee
over there	là-bas	la-ba
owe (to)	devoir	deʳ-vwar
owner	le propriétaire	prop-ree-ay-tair

P

pack (to) *parcel*	emballer	ahⁿ-ba-lay
pack (to) *luggage*	faire les bagages	fair lay ba-gazh
packet	le paquet	pa-kay
page	la page	pazh
pain	la douleur	doo-lœr
paint (to)	peindre	paⁿdr
painting	la peinture	paⁿ-tuᵉr
pair	la paire	pair
palace	le palais/le château	pa-lay/sha-toh

pale	pâle/blême	pal/blem
paper	le papier	pap-yay
parcel	le colis/le paquet	ko-lee/pa-kay
park (to)	stationner	sta-syon-ay
park	le parc	park
part	la partie	par-tee
party	la réception/la soirée	ray-sep-syohⁿ/ swa-ray
pass (to)	passer	pas-ay
passenger (train)	le voyageur	vwa-ya-zhœr
passenger (sea, air)	le passager	pas-azh-ay
passport	le passeport	pas-por
past	(le) passé	pas-ay
path	le sentier	sahⁿ-tyay
patient	le/la malade	ma-lad
pavement	le trottoir	trot-war
pay (to)	payer	pay-ay
pearl	la perle	pairl
pebble	le galet	ga-lay
pedal	la pédale	pay-dal
pedestrian	le piéton	pyay-tohⁿ
pen	le stylo	stee-loh
pencil	le crayon	kray-ohⁿ
penknife	le canif	ka-neef

people	les gens *m*	zhahⁿ
per person	par personne	par pair-son
perfect	parfait	par-fe
performance	la représentation	re^r-pray-zahⁿ-ta-syohⁿ
perfume	le parfum	par-faⁿ
perhaps	peut-être	pe^r-tetr
perishable	périssable	pay-ree-sabl
permit	le permis	pair-mee
permit (to)	permettre	pair-metr
person	la personne	pair-son
personal	personnel	pair-son-el
petticoat	la combinaison	kohⁿ-bee-nay-zoh^a
photograph	la photographie	fo-to-gra-fee
photographer	le photographe	fo-to-graf
piano	le piano	pya-no
pick (to) *gather*	cueillir	kay-yeer
pick (to) *choose*	choisir	shwa-zeer
piece	le morceau	mor-soh
picnic	le pique-nique	peek-neek
pier	la jetée	zhe^r-tay
pillow	l'oreiller *m*	lor-ay-yay
(safety) pin	l'épingle *f* (de sûreté)	lay-paⁿgl (de^r su^er-tay)
pipe	la pipe	peep
pity	la pitié	pee-tyay

place	l'endroit *m*	lah^n-drwa
plain	simple	sa^{n}pl
plan	le plan	plah^n
plant	la plante	plah^{n}t
plastic	le plastique	plas-teek
plate	l'assiette *f*	las-yet
play	la pièce (de théâtre)	pyes (de^r tay-atr)
play (to)	jouer	zhoo-ay
player	le joueur	zhoo-œr
please	s'il vous plaît	seel voo ple
plenty	beaucoup (de)	boh-koo
pliers	les pinces *f*	pa^{n}s
plug	le bouchon	boo-shoh^n
plug (electric)	la prise (électrique)	preez (ay-lek-treek)
pocket	la poche	posh
point	le point	pwa^n
poisonous *animal*	venimeux	ve-nee-mœ
poisonous *plant*	vénéneux	vay-nay-nœ
police station	le poste de police	post de^r po-lees
policeman	l'agent de police *m*	la-zhah^n de^r po-lees
poor	pauvre	pohvr
popular	populaire	po-pu^e-lair
port	le port	por
possible	possible	po-seebl

post (to)	mettre à la poste	metr a la post
post box	la boîte aux lettres	bwat oh letr
post office	le bureau de poste	bue-roh der post
postcard	la carte postale	kart pos-tal
postman	le facteur	fak-tœr
postpone (to)	reporter/remettre	rer-por-tay/rer-metr
pound	la livre	leevr
powder	la poudre	poodr
prefer (to)	préférer	pray-fay-ray
prepare (to)	préparer	pray-par-ay
present *gift*	le cadeau	ka-doh
press (to)	repasser	rer-pas-ay
pretty	joli	zho-lee
price	le prix	pree
priest	le prêtre	pretr
print	l'estampe	les-tahnp
print *photo*	l'épreuve	lay-prerv
print (to)	imprimer	an-pree-may
print (to) *photo*	tirer	tee-ray
private	privé	pree-vay
problem	le problème	pro-blem
profession	la profession	pro-fes-yohn
programme	le programme	pro-gram
promise	la promesse	pro-mes

promise (to)	promettre	pro-metr
prompt	prompt	prohⁿt
protestant	protestant	pro-test-ahⁿ
provide (to)	fournir	foor-neer
public	public	pu^e-bleek
pull (to)	tirer	tee-ray
pump	la pompe	pohⁿp
pure	pur	pu^er
purse	le porte-monnaie	port mo-nay
push (to)	pousser	poo-say
put (to)	mettre	metr
pyjamas	le pyjama	pee-zha-ma

Q

quality	la qualité	kal-ee-tay
quantity	la quantité	kahⁿ-tee-tay
quarter	le quart	kar
queen	la reine	ren
question	la question	kes-tyohⁿ
queue	la file/la queue	feel/ke^r
queue (to)	faire la queue	fair la ke^r
quick(ly)	rapide(ment)	ra-peed(-mahⁿ)

| quiet | tranquille | trahⁿ-keel |
| quite | tout à fait | too-ta-fe |

R

racecourse	l'hippodrome *m*	lee-po-drom
races	les courses *f*	koors
radiator	le radiateur	ra-dya-tœr
radio	la radio	ra-dyoh
railway	le chemin de fer	she^rmaⁿ de^r fair
rain	la pluie	plwee
rain (to)	pleuvoir	plœ-vwar
raincoat	l'imperméable *m*	laⁿ-pair-may-abl
rare	rare	rar
rather	plutôt	plu^e-toh
raw	cru	cru^e
razor	le rasoir	ra-zwar
razor blade	la lame de rasoir	lam de^r ra-zwar
reach (to)	atteindre	a-taⁿdr
read (to)	lire	leer
ready	prêt	pre
real	vrai	vre
really	vraiment	vre-mahⁿ

reason	la raison	re-zoh^n
receipt	le reçu/la quittance	re^r-su^e/kee-tah^{n}s
receive (to)	recevoir	re^r-se^r-vwar
recent	récent	ray-sah^n
recipe	la recette	re^r-set
recognize (to)	reconnaître	re^r-ko-netr
recommend (to)	recommander	re^r-ko-mah^n-day
record *music*	le disque	deesk
record *sport*	le record	re^r-kor
refrigerator	le réfrigérateur	ray-free-zhay-ra-tœr
regards	les compliments *m/* les amitiés *f*	koh^n-plee-mah^n/ a-mee-tyay
register (to)	enregistrer	ah^n-rezh-ees-tray
register (to) *letter*	recommander	re^r-ko-mah^n-day
relatives	les parents	pa-rah^n
religion	la religion	re^r-lee-zhyoh^n
remember (to)	se souvenir (de)	se^r soov-neer
rent	le loyer	lwa-yay
rent (to)	louer	loo-ay
repair (to)	réparer	ray-par-ay
repeat (to)	répéter	ray-pay-tay
reply (to)	répondre	ray-poh^{n}dr
reservation	la réservation	ray-zair-va-syoh^n
reserve (to)	réserver	ray-zair-vay

restaurant	le restaurant	res-tor-ah^n
restaurant car	le wagon-restaurant	va-goh^n res-tor-ah^n
return (to) *come back*	revenir	re^{r}v-neer
return (to) *go back*	retourner	re^r-toor-nay
return (to) *give back*	rendre	rah^{n}dr
reward	la récompense	ray-koh^n-pah^{n}s
ribbon	le ruban	ru^e-bah^n
rich	riche	reesh
ride	la promenade	prom-nad
ride (to) *horse*	monter à cheval	moh^n-tay a she^r-val
right *opp. left*	droit	drwa
right *opp. wrong*	juste	zhu^{e}st
right (to be)	avoir raison	avwar re-zoh^n
ring	la bague	bag
ripe	mûr	mu^{e}r
rise (to)	se lever	se^r le^r-vay
river	le fleuve/la rivière[1]	flœv/reev-yair
road *between towns*	la route	root
road *within towns*	la rue	ru^e
rock	le rocher	ro-shay
roll (to)	rouler	roo-lay
roller *hair*	le rouleau	roo-loh

1. 'Fleuve' is used for rivers that flow into the sea and 'rivière' for rivers that flow into other rivers.

roof	le toit	twa
room	la chambre	shah^{n}br
rope	la corde	kord
rotten	pourri	poo-ree
rough	grossier/rude	groh-syay/ru^{e}d
round	rond	roh^n
rowing boat	le bateau à rames	ba-toh a ram
rubber	caoutchouc	ka-oot-shoo
rubbish	les ordures *f*	lay zor-du^{e}r
rucksack	le sac à dos	sak a doh
rude	grossier	groh-syay
ruin	la ruine	ru^e-een
rule (to)	gouverner	goo-vair-nay
run (to)	courir	koo-reer

S

sad	triste	treest
safe *unharmed*	sauf	sohf
safe *secure*	en sûreté	ah^n su^{e}r-tay
sailor	le marin	ma-ra^n
sale *clearance*	les soldes *m*	sohld
(for) sale	à vendre	a vah^{n}dr
salesman/girl	le vendeur/vendeuse	vah^n-dœr/vah^n-dœz

salt	le sel	sel
salt water	l'eau salée *f*	loh sa-lay
same	le/la même	mem
sand	le sable	sabl
sandal	la sandale	sah^n-dal
sanitary towel	la serviette hygiénique	sair-vyet ee-zhyay-neek
satisfactory	satisfaisant	sa-tees-fe-zah^n
saucer	la soucoupe	soo-koop
save (to)	économiser	ay-ko-no-mee-zay
save (to) *rescue*	sauver	soh-vay
say (to)	dire	deer
scald oneself (to)	s'ébouillanter	say-bwee-yah^n-tay
scarf	le foulard	foo-lar
scenery	le paysage	pay-zazh
scent	le parfum	par-fa^n
school	l'école *f*	lay-kol
scissors	les ciseaux *m*	see-zoh
Scotland	l'Écosse *f*	lay-kos
Scottish	écossais/écossaise	ay-ko-se (-sez)
scratch (to)	égratigner	ay-gra-teen-yay
screw	la vis	vees
sculpture	la sculpture	sku^{e}l-tu^{e}r

sea	la mer	mair
sea food	les fruits de mer *m*	frwee de^r mair
seasickness	le mal de mer	mal de^r mair
season	la saison	se-zoh^n
seat	la place	plas
second	deuxième	de^r-zyem
see (to)	voir	vwar
seem (to)	sembler	sah^n-blay
sell (to)	vendre	vah^n-dr
send (to)	envoyer	ah^n-vwa-yay
separate(ly)	séparé(ment)	say-pa-ray(-mah^n)
serious	sérieux	sayr-ye^r
serve (to)	servir	sair-veer
served	servi	sair-vee
service (charge)	le service	sair-vees
service *church*	l'office *m*	lo-fees
several	plusieurs	plu^e-zyœr
sew (to)	coudre	koodr
shade *colour*	la teinte	ta^{n}t
shade/shadow	l'ombre *f*	loh^{n}br
shallow	peu profond	pe^r pro-foh^n
shampoo	le shampooing	shah^n-pwa^n
shape	la forme	form
share (to)	partager	par-ta-zhay

sharp	aigu/pointu	egu^e/pwa^n-tu^e
shave (to)	se raser	se^r ra-zay
shaving brush	le blaireau	ble-roh
shaving cream	la crème à raser	krem a ra-zay
shaving foam	la mousse à raser	moos a ra-zay
she	elle	el
sheet	le drap	dra
shell	le coquillage	ko-kee-yazh
shelter	l'abri *m*	la-bree
shine (to)	briller	bree-yay
shingle	le galet	ga-lay
ship	la bateau	ba-toh
shipping line	la compagnie de navigation	koh^n-pan-yee de^r na-vee-ga-syoh^n
shirt	la chemise	she^r-meez
shock	le choc	shok
shoe	le soulier/la chaussure	soo-lyay/shoh-su^{e}r
shoe polish	le cirage	see-razh
shoelace	le lacet (de soulier)	la-say
shop	le magasin	ma-ga-za^n
shopping centre	le centre commercial	sah^{n}tr ko-mair-syal
shore	la côte/le rivage	koht/ree-vazh
short	court	koor
shortly	bientôt	byah^n-toh

shorts	le short	short
shoulder	l'épaule *f*	lay-pohl
show *theatre*	le spectacle	spek-takl
show (to)	montrer	moh^n-tray
shower	la douche	doosh
shut *pp*	fermé	fair-may
shut (to)	fermer	fair-may
side	le côté	koh-tay
sights	les monuments *m*	mon-u^e-mah^n
	les curiosités *f*	ku^e-ree-ozee-tay
sightseeing (to go)	visiter les monuments	vee-zee-tay lay mon-u^e-mah^n
sign	le signe	seen-y
sign (to)	signer	seen-yay
signpost	le panneau indicateur	pa-noh a^n-dee-ka-tœr
silver	l'argent *m*	lar-zhah^n
simple	simple	sa^{n}pl
since	depuis	de^r-pwee
sing (to)	chanter	shah^n-tay
single	seul	sœl
single room	la chambre pour une personne	shah^{n}br poor u^{e}n pair-son
sister	la sœur	sœr
sit down (to)	s'asseoir	sas-war
sitting	assis	asee

size	la grandeur/la taille	grah^n-doer/ta-y
skate (to)	patiner	pa-tee-nay
skating	le patinage	pa-tee-nazh
ski (to)	skier	skee-ay
skid (to)	déraper	day-rap-ay
skiing	le ski	skee
skirt	la jupe	zhu^{e}p
sky	le ciel	sy-el
sleep (to)	dormir	dor-meer
sleeper	le wagon-lit	va-goh^n lee
sleeping bag	le sac de couchage	sak de^r koo-shazh
sleeve	la manche	mah^{n}sh
slice	la tranche	trah^{n}sh
slip	la combinaison	koh^n-bee-ne-zoh^n
slipper	la pantoufle	pah^n-toofl
slow(ly)	lent(ement)	lah^n(-te^r-mah^n)
small	petit	pe^r-tee
smart	chic	sheek
smell	l'odeur f	loh-dœr
smell (to)	sentir	sah^n-teer
smile (to)	sourire	soo-reer
smoke (to)	fumer	fu^e-may
smoking compartment	le compartment fumeur	koh^n-par-tee-mah^n fu^e-mœr

(no) smoking	défense de fumer	day-fahⁿs deʳ fueᵉ-may
snow	la neige	nezh
snow (to)	neiger	nezh-ay
so	si	see
soap	le savon	sav-ohⁿ
soap powder	le savon en paillettes	sav-ohⁿ ahⁿ pa-yet
sober	pas ivre	pa-zeevr
sock	la chaussette	shoh-set
soft	mou/molle; doux/douce	moo/mol; doo/doos
sold	vendu	vahⁿ-dueᵉ
sole *shoe*	la semelle	seʳ-mel
solid	solide	so-leed
some	quelque	kel-keʳ
somebody	quelqu'un	kel-keⁿ
something	quelque chose	kel-keʳ-shohz
sometimes	quelquefois	kel-keʳ-fwa
somewhere	quelque part	kel-keʳ par
son	le fils	fees
song	la chanson	shahⁿ-sohⁿ
soon	bientôt	byaⁿ-toh
sort	l'espèce *f*	les-pes
sound	le bruit/le son	brwee/sohⁿ
sour	aigre	egr

south	le sud	sue<d
souvenir	le souvenir	soov-neer
space	l'espace *m*	les-pas
spanner	la clé	klay
spare	de réserve/de rechange	de<r ray-zairv/de<r re<r-shah<nzh
speak (to)	parler	par-lay
speciality	la spécialité	spay-syal-ee-tay
spectacles	les lunettes *f*	lu<e-net
speed	la vitesse	vee-tes
speed limit	la limitation de vitesse	lee-mee-ta-syoh<n de<r vee-tes
spend (to) *money*	dépenser	day-pah<n-say
spend (to) *time*	passer	pa-say
spoon	la cuiller	kwee-yay
sport	le sport	spor
sprain (to)	se fouler	see foo-lay
spring *water*	la source	soors
square *adj*	carré	ka-ray
square *in town*	la place	plas
stables	les écuries	ay-kue<e-ree
stage	la scène	sen
stain	la tache	tash
stained	taché	ta-shay

stairs	l'escalier *m*	les-kal-yay
stalls	les fauteuils d'orchestre *m*	foh-tœ-y dor-kestr
stamp	le timbre	ta^{n}br
stand (to)	se tenir debout	se^r te^r-neer de^r-boo
star	l'étoile *f*	lay-twal
start (to)	commencer	ko-mah^n-say
statue	la statue	sta-tu^e
stay (to)	rester	res-tay
step	le pas	pa
steward *airline*	le steward	stew-ar
steward *ship*	le garçon de cabine	gar-soh^n de^r ka-been
stewardess	l'hotesse	loh-tes
stick	le bâton	ba-toh^n
stiff	dur/raide	du^{e}r/red
still *not moving*	immobile	ee-mo-beel
still *time*	toujours/encore	too-zhoor/ah^n-kor
sting	la piqûre	pee-ku^{e}r
stocking	le bas	ba
stolen	volé	vo-lay
stone	la pierre	py-air
stool	le tabouret	ta-boo-ray
stop (to)	s'arrêter	sa-re-tay
store	le magasin	ma-ga-za^n

storm	l'orage m/la tempete	lor-azh/tah^n-pet
stove	le réchaud	ray-shoh
straight	droit	drwa
straight on	tout droit	too drwa
strange	étrange	ay-trah^{n}zh
strap	la courroie	koor-wa
stream	le ruisseau	rwee-soh
street	la rue	ru^e
stretch (to)	tendre/s'étendre	tah^{n}dr/say-tah^{n}dr
string	la ficelle	fee-sel
strong	fort	for
student	l'étudiant(e)	lay-tu^e-dyah^n(t)
stung (to be)	être piqué	etr pee-kay
style	le style	steel
subject	le sujet	su^e-zhay
suburb	la banlieue	ba^n-lye^r
subway	le passage souterrain	pa-sazh soo-ter-a^n
such	tel/pareil	tel/pa-ray
suede	le daim	da^n
suggestion	la suggestion	su^e-zhes-tyoh^n
suit *men*	le costume	kos-tu^{e}m
suit *women*	le tailleur	ta-yœr
suitcase	la valise	va-leez
sun	le soleil	so-lay

sunbathe (to)	se bronzer	se^r brohⁿ-zay
	prendre un bain de soleil	prahⁿdr eⁿ baⁿ de^r sol-ay
sunburn	le coup de soleil	koo de^r sol-ay
sunglasses	les lunettes de soleil *f*	lu^e-net de^r sol-ay
sunhat	le chapeau de paille	sha-poh de^e pa-y
sunny	ensoleillé	ahⁿ-sol-ay-yay
sunshade	l'ombrelle *f*	lom-brel
suntan oil	l'huile solaire *f*	lweel sol-air
supper	le souper	soo-pay
sure	sûr	su^er
surgery/surgery hours	le cabinet/les heures de consultation	ka-bee-nay/œr de^r kon-su^el-ta-syohⁿ
surprise	la surprise	su^er-preez
surprise (to)	surprendre	su^er-prahⁿdr
suspender belt	le porte-jarretelles	port zhar-tel
sweat	la sueur	su^e-œr
sweater	le sweater	swe-tair
sweet *adj*	sucré	su^e-kray
sweet	le bonbon	bohⁿ-bohⁿ
swell (to)	enfler	ahⁿ-flay
swim (to)	nager	na-zhay
swimming pool	la piscine	pee-seen
swings	les balançoires *f*	ba-lahⁿ-swar

Swiss	suisse	swees
switch *light*	l'interrupteur *m*	lan-tay-rue p-tœr
Switzerland	la Suisse	swees
synagogue	la synagogue	see-na-gog

T

table	la table	tabl
tablecloth	la nappe	nap
tablet	le comprimé	kohn-pree-may
tailor	le tailleur	ta-yœr
take (to)	prendre	prahndr
talk (to)	parler	par-lay
tall	grand	grahn
tank	le réservoir	ray-zair-vwar
tanned	bronzé	brohn-zay
tap	le robinet	ro-bee-nay
taste	le goût	goo
taste (to)	goûter	goo-tay
tax	la taxe/l'impot *m*	taks/lan-po
taxi	le taxi	tak-see
taxi rank	la station de taxis	sta-syohn der tak-see
teach (to)	enseigner	ahn-sen-yay

tear	la déchirure	day-shee-ru^er
tear (to)	déchirer	day-shee-ray
telegram	le télégramme	tay-lay-gram
telephone	le téléphone	tay-lay-fon
telephone (to)	téléphoner	tay-lay-fon-ay
telephone box	la cabine téléphonique	ka-been tay-lay-fon-eek
telephone call	le coup de téléphone	koo de^r tay-lay-fon
telephone directory	l'annuaire *m*	la-nue-air
telephone number	le numéro de téléphone	nue-may-roh de^r tay-lay-fon
telephone operator	le/la standardiste	stah^n-dar-deest
telephone token	le jeton (de téléphone)	zhe^r-toh^n
television	la télévision	tay-lay-vee-zyoh^n
tell (to)	dire	deer
temperature	la témperature	tah^n-pay-ra-tu^er
temple *church*	le temple	tah^npl
temporary	temporaire	tah^n-por-air
tennis	le tennis	te-nees
tent	la tente	tah^nt
tent peg	le piquet (de tente)	pee-kay
tent pole	le montant (de tente)	moh^n-tah^n
terrace	la terrasse	ter-as
than	que	ke^r

that	cela	sla
the	le/la/les	le^r, la, lay
theatre	le théâtre	tay-atr
their(s)	leur	lœr
them	les/leur/eux	lay/lœr/e^r
then	alors	alor
there	là	la
there is/are	il y a	eel-ya
thermometer	le thermomètre	tair-mom-etr
these	ces	say
they	ils/elles	eel/el
thick	épais	ay-pe
thin	mince	ma^{n}s
thing	la chose	shohz
think (to)	penser	pah^n-say
thirsty (to be)	avoir soif	av-war swaf
this	ce/cet/cette	se^r/set/set
those	ces	say
though	quoique	kwa-ke^r
thread	le fil	feel
through	à travers/par	a tra-vair/par
throw (to)	lancer/jeter	lah^n-say/zhe^r-tay
thunderstorm	l'orage *m*	lor-azh
ticket	le billet	bee-yay

tide	la marée	ma-ray
tie	la cravate	kra-vat
tie *sport*	le match nul	match nu^{el}
tight	serré	se-ray
tights	un collant	ko-lahⁿ
time	le temps/l'heure *f*	tahⁿ/lœr
timetable	l'horaire *m*	lor-air
tin	la boîte	bwat
tin opener	l'ouvre-boîte *m*	loovr bwat
tip	le pourboire	poor-bwar
tired (to be)	(être) fatigué	(etr) fa-tee-gay
to	à/pour	a/poor
tobacco	le tabac	ta-bak
tobacco pouch	la blague à tabac	blag a ta-bak
together	ensemble	ahⁿ-sahⁿbl
toilet	la toilette	twa-let
toilet paper	le papier hygiénique	pap-yay ee-zhyay-neek
tongue	la langue	lahⁿg
too *also*	aussi	oh-see
too, too much/many	trop (de)	troh
toothbrush	la brosse à dents	bros a dahⁿ
toothpaste	la pâte dentifrice	pat dahⁿ-tee-frees
toothpick	le cure-dents	ku^er-dahⁿ
top	le sommet	som-may

torch	la lampe (de poche)	lahⁿp
torn	déchiré	day-shee-ray
touch (to)	toucher	too-shay
tough	dur	duᵉr
tour	le tour/la visite	toor/vee-zeet
tourist	le touriste	toor-eest
towards	vers	vair
towel	la serviette	sair-vyet
tower	la tour	toor
town	la ville	veel
town hall	l'hôtel de ville *m*	lo-tel deʳ veel
toy	le jouet	zhoo-ay
traffic	la circulation	seer-kuᵉ-la-syohⁿ
traffic jam	l'embouteillage *m*	lahⁿ-boo-tay-azh
traffic lights	les feux *m*	feʳ
trailer	la remorque	reʳ-mork
train	le train	traⁿ
tram	le tram	tram
transfer (to)	changer	shahⁿ-zhay
transit	le transit	trahⁿ-zeet
translate (to)	traduire	tra-dweer
travel (to)	voyager	vwa-ya-zhay
travel agency	l'agence de voyage *f*	la-zhahⁿs deʳ vwa-yazh
traveller	le voyageur	vwa-ya-zhœr

traveller's cheque	le chèque de voyage	shek de^r vwa-yazh
treat (to)	traiter	tre-tay
treatment	le traitement	tret-mah^n
tree	l'arbre m	larbr
trip	l'excursion f	lek-sku^{e}r-syoh^n
trouble	les ennuis m	lay-zah^n-nwee
trousers	le pantalon	pah^n-ta-loh^n
true	vrai	vre
trunk *luggage*	la malle	mal
trunks	le caleçon	kal-soh^n
truth	la vérité	vay-ree-tay
try, try on (to)	essayer	esay-yay
tunnel	le tunnel	tu^e-nel
turn (to)	tourner	toor-nay
turning	le tournant	toor-nah^n
tweezers	les pinces (à épiler) f	pa^{n}s (a ay-pee-lay)
twin beds	les lits jumeaux	lee zhu^e-moh
twisted	tordu	tor-du^e

ugly	laid	le
umbrella	le parapluie	para-plwee
(beach) umbrella	le parasol	para-sol

uncle	l'oncle *m*	loh^nkl
uncomfortable	mal à l'aise	mal al-ez
under	sous	soo
underground	le métro	may-troh
underneath	sous	soo
understand	comprendre	koh^n-prah^ndr
underwater fishing	la pêche sous-marine	pesh soo ma-reen
underwear	les sous-vêtements *m*	soo vet-mah^n
university	l'université *f*	lu^e-nee-vair-see-tay
unpack (to)	défaire les bagages	day-fair lay bag-azh
until	jusqu'à	zhu^es-ka
unusual	peu commun	per kom-e^n
up (stairs)	en haut	ah^n-oh
urgent	urgent	u^er-zhah^n
us	nous	noo
U.S.A.	les États-Unis	lay-zay-ta-zu^e-nee
use (to)	utiliser	u^e-tee-lee-zay
	se servir (de)	se^r sair-veer
useful	utile	u^e-teel
useless	inutile	ee-nu^e-teel
usual	habituel/ordinaire	a-bee-tu^e-el/or-dee-nair

V

vacancies	chambres libres *f*	shah^{n}br leebr
vacant	libre	leebr
vacation	les vacances *f*	va-kah^{n}s
valid	valable	va-labl
valley	la vallée	va-lay
valuable	précieux	pray-sye^r
value	la valeur	va-lœr
vase	le vase	vahz
vegetable	le légume	lay-gu^{e}m
vegetarian	le végétarien	vay-zhay-ta-rya^n
ventilation	l'aération	la-ay-ra-syoh^n
very	très	tre
very little	très peu	tre pe^r
very much	beaucoup	boh-koo
vest	le maillot	ma-yo
view	la vue	vu^e
villa	la villa	vee-la
village	le village	vee-lazh
violin	le violon	vyo-loh^n
visa	le visa	vee-za
visibility	la visibilité	vee-zee-bee-lee-tay
visit	la visite	vee-zeet

visit (to) *place*	visiter	vee-zee-tay
voice	la voix	vwa
voltage	le voltage	vol-tazh
voyage	le voyage	vwa-yazh

wait (to)	attendre	at-ahⁿdr
waiter	le garçon	gar-sohⁿ
waiting room	la salle d'attente	sal da-tahⁿt
waitress	la serveuse	sair-vœz
wake (to)	se réveiller	seʳ ray-vay-ay
Wales	le Pays de Galles	pay-ee deʳ gal
walk	la promenade	prom-nad
walk (to)	marcher/se promener	mar-shay/seʳ prom-nay
wall	le mur	muᵉr
wall plug	la prise	preez
wallet	le portefeuille	port-fœ-y
want (to)	vouloir/avoir besoin (de)	vool-war/avwar beʳ-zwaⁿ
wardrobe	l'armoire *f*	lar-mwar
warm	chaud	shoh
wash (to)	laver	la-vay
washbasin	le lavabo	la-va-boh

waste	le gaspillage	gas-pee-yazh
waste (to)	gaspiller	gas-pee-yay
watch	la montre	moh^{n}tr
water (fresh/salt)	l'eau f (douce/salée)	loh (doos/sa-lay)
water ski(-ing)	le ski nautique	skee noh-teek
waterfall	la chute d'eau	shu^{e}t doh
waterproof	imperméable	a^n-pair-may-abl
wave sea	la vague	vag
way	le chemin	she^{r}ma^n
we	nous	noo
wear (to)	porter	por-tay
weather	le temps	tah^n
week	la semaine	se^r-men
weigh (to)	peser	pe^r-say
weight	le poids	pwa
welcome	bienvenu	bya^n-ve-nu^e
well	bien	bya^n
Welsh	gallois/galloise	gal-wa (-waz)
west	l'ouest m	lwest
wet	mouillé	mwee-yay
what?	quel/quelle?	kel
wheel	la roue	roo
when?	quand?	kah^n
where?	où?	oo

whether	si	see
which?	quel(s)/quelle(s)?	kel
while	pendant que	pahⁿ-dahⁿ ke^r
who?	qui?	kee
whole	le tout	too
whose?	à qui?	a kee
why?	pourquoi?	poor-kwa
wide	large	larzh
widow	la veuve	vœv
widower	le veuf	vœf
wife	la femme	fam
wild	sauvage	soh-vazh
win (to)	gagner	gan-yay
wind	le vent	vahⁿ
window	la fenêtre	fe^r-netr
wing	l'aile *f*	lel
wire	le fil de fer	feel de^r fer
wish (to)	souhaiter	swe-tay
with	avec	avek
within	dans/à l'intérieur	dahⁿ/a-laⁿ-tay-ryœr
without	sans	sahⁿ
woman	la femme	fam
wood	le bois	bwa
wool	la laine	len

word	le mot	moh
work	le travail	tra-vy
work (to)	travailler	tra-vy-yay
worry (to)	s'inquiéter	saⁿ-kye-tay
worse	pire	peer
worth (to be)	valoir	val-war
wrap (to)	envelopper	ahⁿ-vlop-ay
write (to)	écrire	ay-kreer
writing paper	le papier à lettre	pap-yay a letr
wrong	mauvais/incorrect	moh-ve/aⁿ-kor-ekt
wrong (to be)	avoir tort	avwar tor

Y

yacht	le yacht/le bateau à voile	yot/ba-toh a vwal
year	l'an *m*/l'année *f*	lahⁿ/la-nay
yet	encore	ahⁿ-kor
yet *nevertheless*	pourtant	poor-tahⁿ
you	vous	voo
young	jeune	zhœn
your	votre *s*/vos *pl*	votr/voh
yours	le/la vôtre	vohtr
youth hostel	l'auberge de jeunesse *f*	loh-bairzh deʳ zhœ-nes

Z

zip	la fermeture éclair	fair-me^r-tu^{e}r ay-klair
zoo	le zoo	zoh

Index